# NAPOLEON

## *In His Own Words*

FROM THE FRENCH OF

JULES BERTAUT

*Translated by Herbert Edward Law*
*and Charles Lincoln Rhodes*

*Authorized Edition*

CHICAGO
A. C. McCLURG & CO.
1916

Published June, 1916





W. F. HALL PRINTING COMPANY, CHICAGO

NAPOLEON IN HIS OWN WORDS

N
N
NAPOLEON

# CONTENTS

# AUTHOR'S PREFACE

THIS collection of Napoleonic aphorisms is not the first attempt of the kind that has been made. The genius of Napoleon has always challenged the attention of historians, as it has that of the unpretending curious and lovers of strong and beautiful maxims; and following the Restoration, as after the rebirth of Imperialism under Napoleon III, there were those who diligently collected these odds and ends of the Emperor's thoughts. However, if this attempt to popularize these reflections of genius is not entirely new, I do not think any other has been undertaken with the same care and candor.

We are now sufficiently distant from Napoleon to judge him with the dispassionateness of an age appreciative, but careful to do justice. And just because there is little concerning this great man which is not now known, we are able to classify in a systematic way the products of his mind. Without attempting a too rigid classification, therefore, I have attempted to present the diverse aspects of the Napoleonic mentality, and to view him successively in his character of professor of psychology and morals, of politics and administration; as an authority on love and marriage; as a patron of the arts; as a soldier and as a sociologist.

The first thing that strikes one in reading these thoughts, these sentiments, these maxims, is the constant concern for sovereign authority which they reveal.

Napoleon, in imagination, was constantly concerned with the good of his subjects. Whether in his literary works, properly so called, or in his immense correspondence or in his conversation or in his public speeches or in his St. Helena confidences, he has taken occasion to express himself on a multitude of problems touching religion, science, morals, art, politics and sociology. And always he does it as a sovereign, as a master conscious of his authority, obsessed with the weight of his extraordinary responsibility and of the duty that devolved upon him.

Only rarely is his attention swerved from

the attainment of the final solution of a social or moral problem. Almost always a sure instinct brings him back to the steadfast aim of his efforts, and these efforts, when they are analyzed, have no other aim than a transcendental utilitarianism. To bring to bear constantly throughout every foot of the Empire, in every soul under his authority, the powers of all for the aggrandizement and prosperity of the nation, that was his unheralded but real anxiety and purpose. To compel every citizen to render all that he is capable of rendering of social usefulness, to drag from men, in spite of themselves and by an iron compulsion, all that they possess of moral wealth and influence, to watch unceasingly the play of institutions and their machinery, from their simplest to their most intricate mechanism, that nothing fail of the particular work assigned to it — that was his constant purpose.

We need not be astonished therefore if this obsession constantly betrays itself in the seemingly unrelated subjects of psychology and morals. Nor ought we to be surprised to find among aphorisms relating to love, this opinion of Napoleon concerning women: "The most important woman in the world, living or dead, is the one who has borne the most children;" or among those concerning Christianity, "The Christian religion will always be the firmest support of every government clever enough to make it serve it;" or among those concerning art, "Tragedy is the school of genius; it is the duty of sovereigns to encourage and support it;" or again, "Books are too argumentative not to corrupt a people by dishabituating it from fact."

These are the beliefs of a sovereign who gives his thought chiefly to the play and interplay of men and things on the stability and power of the state. Truth never appears naked to such a mind; she is always more or less draped. He never sees truth objectively, but always in relation to some one or some thing.

But what, in the last analysis, is this utilitarianism which is the essence of Napoleon's genius? It is, in a word, the art of adaptation carried to its highest expression. To know how to create "the man for the place," as the trenchant English saying has it, and to get the supremest possible out of him — such is the whole secret of the Napoleonic necromancy. This genius requires for its highest exercise certain qualities which the Emperor possessed in the maximum of intensity.

In the first place he had an extraordinary gift of insight. Napoleon was first of all a dissector of souls — that is easily seen in running through the chapter on psychology and that on politics. It is evident also in the maxims collected under the title "Administration."

Let us reflect that he had lived through the most astounding years of history, those during which the human heart revealed itself in all its nakedness; that he had known things at their worst, and seen at close range the most sinister souls. But his knowledge of the human being was not only of a rigorous exactitude, he also knew the deep furrows which nationality plows in temperament; and, in particular, some of the judgments of the French character he has expressed have the quality of finality.

Moreover his insight has no tinge of cruelty. He was himself too quivering with life to linger a pessimist at the spectacle of humanity. On the other hand he visions too clearly not to take advantage at once of what he sees or to profit by his experience. For example, he observes that, "Men are greedy for emotion," and he adds at once, "their enthusiasm is his who can cleverly arouse it." He says, "It is important to recognize human weakness," but he exclaims as a conclusion, "and turn it to your advantage rather than to oppose it." Thus always, in him, policy followed close on psychology.

But keen insight alone is not sufficient to continually fit men for the places to be filled. It does not suffice to recognize ability in men; it is necessary to inspire them. Following insight, comes guidance. That is the difficult thing. No mind was more single in its will, no energy more irresistible than his. With him, to form a purpose was to execute it. His mind could conceive of neither obstacles from within nor from without which could swerve it. While his prudence might suggest temporary yielding to circumstances, he avowed it with a sort of superior artlessness: "Pretexts never fail the man who has the power to do what he pleases." However, read and re-read these aphorisms — those which are the fruit of long experience, as his maxims of war, those which were the spontaneous outburst of the moment, or those which were the result of ripened thought — the positive way he says them gives them the seal of authenticity.

But in addition to the power of insight, and the gift of authority, a certain recognition of the supremacy of moral ideas was necessary thoroughly to understand the citizen-subjects of the Empire, and to foresee how they would adjust themselves to any given set of conditions. The Emperor recognized this supremacy of moral ideas; not as a deep and abiding conviction, nor as a superstitious belief. The man who said that a monarch ought to be acquainted with all religions in order to be ready, on occasion, to embrace them all, had but a modicum of superstition, moral or religious. But here, again, Napoleon's instinct for policy came into play, and he realized that any empire in which sound moral principles, were not given free scope, was bound to fall.

For him, therefore, outwardly to conform to morality, to preach morality, to defend it, and to impose it on men and to require it of them by all possible means, was merely calculation. The result of it he intended should be, everywhere and always, a realization of the thought expressed by that character in Italian comedy who is made to say, "I will make you happy in spite of yourselves." Similarly, Napoleon might have said to his subjects, "I will make you moral, religious, and honest in spite of yourselves," adding to himself, "because such is to the supreme interest of the Empire."

Every means is good to him which will firmly fix these truths in the French mind; and he uses all means with consummate adroitness. When the Grenadier Gobin committed suicide for love, Napoleon at once addressed his troops thus: "A soldier ought to overcome the melancholy and bitterness of hopeless passion; to abandon himself to disappointment without resistance, to kill himself in order to escape from himself, is to abandon the field of battle without gaining the victory." Thus he shows by example to those willing to see it, that moral qualities are indispensable; and Napoleon knew how to utilize all means to arouse them. Thus was strengthened in each soul the conviction that, in proportion to his ability, it was the duty of each citizen to cooperate for the grandeur and prosperity of the country represented in the person of the Emperor.

Such are the qualities indispensable to one, who, through a supreme utilitarianism would fashion men in his own image and make of them the instruments of his domination. But important as these qualities are, obvious as it is that they should be found in a sovereign, they are still insufficient to accomplish supreme results. There must be added to them a sense of harmony, an artistic instinct for the sculpture and design of the monument to be raised, a searching vigilance careful of the smallest details, leaving nothing to chance; in a word, that sense of form which Napoleon possessed in the highest degree, and which makes him kin to the world's great artists.

I recall M. Paul Bourget, one day, in one of those satisfying conversations in which he excelled, developing the theory, that, as the Emperor's family was of Tuscan origin one would expect to find in him an artistic sense, an appreciation of form, an inherited sense of balance and harmony. And this indeed it is easy to recognize in his work, which though a little massive, perhaps, is admirably proportioned.

This impression is never so vividly presented to my mind as in considering the minute care for the smallest details, with which Napoleon occupied himself with an untiring passion. In his maxims regarding war there will be found one which is extremely characteristic in this respect. It is where he is speaking of a commanding general's addresses to his troops, and of the necessity of issuing them on the day before the battle or the day before that. "It is not," he says, "that addresses to an army at the moment of action make soldiers brave; their usefulness lies in their effect on the course of the campaign, in neutralizing rumors, and in furnishing matter for camp-fire talk." What a keen and comprehensive understanding of camp life this last phrase reveals! And it is strikingly typical, as it is suggestive, of that creative imagination which enabled Napoleon to foresee and estimate the action and reaction of things and of words, to their most distant consequences. The care for detail is there, and whoever possesses it to this degree is born to achievement, no matter in what direction his activities lead him.

These, it seems to me, are some of the conclusions this book has to suggest. There is no pretense that it gives a new presentation of Napoleon, his qualities or his defects; but it will serve to recall and fix in the memory some of those utterances, which, after a hundred years, still describe the social order, and which are the fruits of a mind which gained them at a cost entitling them to be called experience.

JULES BERTAUT

## TRANSLATORS' PREFACE

IT is now almost exactly a hundred years since Waterloo. Every one of those years has seen additions to the ever-growing volume of Napoleonic literature. Opinion regarding Napoleon is gradually becoming clarified, as more and more the truth of history is being separated from the interests, the passions, and the limitations of knowledge which have obscured it in the past.

This collection of Napoleon's sayings, which M. Jules Bertaut has presented under the title of *Virilities,* is one of the latest, as in some respects it is one of the most important, of late contributions to the subject. It is not that he has discovered new facts about Napoleon. As he says himself, there is probably little that concerns Napoleon which is not now known. Because this is so, we have been able to see Napoleon in the light of fairly complete knowledge of contemporaneous conditions. But what

M. Bertaut has done, is to enable us to see, as it were, through Napoleon's own eyes. We are able otherwise to know what Napoleon did, and what were the circumstances that influenced him. But herein M. Bertaut has given us, in brief, it is true, and by illustration rather than in complete detail, what Napoleon said about the things he did, the reasons he gave for doing them (which are often only the reasons he wanted believed), and the purposes he had in mind.

It is true that there is nothing in this collection of Napoleon's sayings which has not been published somewhere before in the collected editions of his orders, his correspondence, or his formal works. But they are collated and made available here; and they have this advantage over any similar previous collection, that in making them, M. Bertaut has had all the advantage of the fuller knowledge we have of Napoleon than any previous generation has had. Precisely because little that concerns Napoleon is now unknown, M. Bertaut has been able to make his selections from the great mass of Napoleon's utterances in such a way as to present most fully and clearly, within the limits of space determined on, the workings of Napoleon's mind — to get whatever light on his character and motives his own words can throw.

This work was well received by the French people on its publication shortly before the outbreak of the present war; and so it is believed it will be of interest to Americans.

In translating, the effort has been made to present Napoleon's thought in its English garb so as to convey the sense that Napoleon's forceful, nervous, though not always accurate French, conveys to French readers.

In the notes, nothing more has been attempted than to put the average American reader on an equal footing, as to allusion and reference to matters of French history or French literature or French experience, with the average French reader, as we may assume him to be. It is only natural to suppose that the average French reader has such a degree of familiarity with these as will enable him to catch, understandingly, Napoleon's allusions to them; just as the average American reader would be able to catch, understandingly, equivalent allusions and reference to our own history and literature. Hence the notes are confined, with at most one or two exceptions, to matters of French history or literature or national experience. As to allusions to men or things of other countries or peoples, it is assumed that the average American reader is already on an equal footing, as to them, with the French reader.

It has been attempted to give to American readers just what M. Bertaut has given to his countrymen.

HERBERT EDWARD LAW
CHARLES LINCOLN RHODES

# THE CHARACTER OF NAPOLEON

NAPOLEON was a man of action. His mind was cast in that mould which sees in events, not the relations they bear to each other as parts of a universe, but their possibilities to him who can seize them for his own benefit. His was not a contemplative mind; he neither looked for, nor studied, the causes of things, but the effects. He has therefore written no philosophy, though much cynical wisdom. Nor did he speak or write to set men thinking, but to influence their actions.

Though a man of action, few have written more than he did. His correspondence, in thirty-two volumes, the publication of which was begun in 1858, is only a part of the recorded mass of ideas which came from his mind. What is included in this little book is, therefore, but the merest fragment of what there was to choose from.

But because Napoleon's mind and character were of the cast and turn that they were, what is here given will better serve its purpose than would a much larger measure of any other man's writings in regard to that man.

Whoever expects to find consistency, or continuity, in what Napoleon has written, will be disappointed, because Napoleon had no profound convictions to weave themselves like golden threads in the web of his acts or his words. He was neither a philosopher developing a system of philosophy, nor a publicist seeking to guide the course of events in accordance with an underlying and permeating, but consistent body of philosophical or scientific laws. He spoke or wrote for the immediate effect of his words, not for their future, or ultimate effect; nor did he concern himself with any niceties of consistency.

Being a man of action, he was constantly doing things. To make the things he did best serve the purpose for which he did them, he felt called on, or found it convenient, to give some reason or explanation for doing them. He was guided in the reason or explanation he gave, not by his real reason or purpose, but by what he thought would serve him best at the time. Naturally, there could be neither consistency nor continuity in it. There was in it, however, himself, the mirror and reflection of both his moral and his mental character.

It is because of this characteristic of Napoleon's utterances, that a selection from his writings, such as this of M. Bertaut's, can have, and does have, a real and an effective value. Few great men can be appraised by samples of their writings. This is particularly true of those whose greatness consists in their gift of ideas or good works to the world. But Napoleon's greatness was in his genius for coordination, for accomplishment. It included, of course, the power to vision great things — great in their magnitude and in the power required to bring them about. But this accomplishment added nothing, or little to the world's store. His combinations were of what already existed, and though incomparably great and marvelous exhibitions of the power of the human mind to do, they created nothing;

and though he conquered half of Europe he left France no bigger than he found it.

And so Napoleon's writings are no measure of the man, because they neither express his thought, nor measure his greatness. His thought was expressed in action, and his greatness in accomplishment. But his writings do express his estimate of moral relationships and of mankind. Moral obligations he looked on as superstitions, useful in holding the world in order for the benefit of himself or anyone else, who, free from such superstitions, was able to exploit it. His estimate of mankind was of creatures obeying certain impulses and susceptible to certain kinds of stimulus, and therefore very suitable for the use and diversion of one, who, like himself, knew how to use and control them.

It is these things, these qualities, that his writings present. Unconsciously he has betrayed himself in them. What was said for its immediate effect, becomes a measure of ulterior motive. Just as astronomers deduce from the aberrations in the movements of the planets the laws of the sidereal universe, so, from the inconsistencies and contradictions of his recorded utterances can be clearly deduced the dominating motives of his acts.

The great defect of Napoleon's character was that he had no profound convictions of duty or obligation or right; at any rate, no profound convictions commensurate with his intellectual powers. Therefore he had nothing to guide him in the selection of objects for accomplishment except the lust and greed of power to do, which grew with the growth, through exercise and experience, of that power. That is why there is so much that is inexplicable particularly in the later years of his career. He is ever urged on by the unsatisfied power of accomplishment, without having profound moral convictions to guide him either in the choice of aim or means.

In this selection from Napoleon's recorded utterances, insignificant and fragmentary as it is as compared with the whole volume of them, can be seen clearly this lack of profound convictions. In their place are cynical half-truths, clever sophistry, self-deception, because the depth and soundness of the moral sense in mankind is unrealized by Napoleon. It is because his writings do not represent or measure his accomplishment, but do represent the quality of his moral fiber, that Napoleon can, in this respect, be appraised by sample; and this collection which M. Bertaut has made is an excellent sample.

H. E. L.
C. L. R.

# NAPOLEON IN HIS OWN WORDS

# NAPOLEON

## *In His Own Words*

---

### I

#### ON SUCCESS

A PRINCE, criticised by his subjects, should never attempt to justify himself to them.

Collective crimes incriminate no one.

The code of health for nations is not that for individuals.

A sovereign ought always to confiscate publicity for his own profit.

There are only two forces that unite men — fear and interest. All great revolutions originate in fear, for the play of interests does not lead to accomplishment.

Audacity succeeds as often as it fails; in life it has an even chance.

The superior man is never in anyone's way.

Profit by the favors of Fortune while her caprices favor you; fear only that she will change out of spite; she is a woman.

Who saves his country violates no law.

Men, like paintings, need a favorable day.

There are so many laws that no one is safe from hanging.

Success is the most convincing talker in the world.

As a rule it is circumstances that make men.

Impatience is a great obstacle to success; he who treats everything with brusqueness gathers nothing, or only immature fruit which will never ripen.

Men are like numerals — they are given value by their position.

Second-rate men, however ambitious, have only commonplace ideas.

When a man is a favorite of Fortune she never takes him unawares, and, however astonishing her favors may be, she finds him ready.

One must indeed be ignorant of the methods of genius to suppose that it allows itself to be cramped by forms. Forms are for mediocrity, and it is fortunate that mediocrity can act only according to routine. Ability takes its flight unhindered.

No one can disguise to himself the fact that a dead man is nothing more than a dead man, and a living man of the slightest pretensions is stronger than the dead man's memory. When a great man dies, one who has rendered high service to his country, the first feeling experienced is one of satisfaction; a weight has been removed; ambitions are freed *(See Note 1).* We may weep a year afterwards when agitations distract the country; but in the first access of feeling there is not even a tinge of regret; last wishes are unconsidered.

Conquerors should know the genius and the language of every religion. They ought to be Moslems in Egypt and Catholics in France, to the extent, at least, of giving sympathetic protection.

The publication of false news is a petty means of producing important effects, but one of which even cool heads cannot foretell the exact results, since each one to whom such news comes interprets it in accordance with his prejudices and his partisanship.

In the eyes of empire builders men are not men, but instruments.

Equality exists only in theory.

The secret of the power to command is to be strong, because in strength there is neither error nor illusion; it is truth in all its nakedness.

Men are more easily governed through their vices than through their virtues.

Correctly analyzed, political liberty is a convenient fable invented by governments to lull the governed.

The torment of precautions often exceeds the dangers to be avoided. It is sometimes better to abandon one's self to destiny.

A sovereign obliged to respect the law may be contributing to the loss of his realm.

A legislature is a serviceable means of obtaining from a people what the king might not dare ask of them.

Nothing has ever been established except by the sword.

Noisy festivals are a necessity. Blockheads love noise, and the multitude are blockheads.

The heart of a statesman should be in his head.

A new-born government must dazzle.

In planning one's course in life, we should always reserve the right to laugh tomorrow at the ideas of yesterday.

Never depend on the multitude, full of instability and whims; always take precautions against it.

Events all hang by a hair. The clever man profits by everything, neglecting nothing that may give him any advantage. The less clever, by slighting some seeming trifle, loses all.

From triumph to downfall is but a step. I have seen a trifle decide the most important issues in the gravest affairs.

It is only by prudence, wisdom, and dexterity, that great ends are attained and obstacles overcome. Without these qualities nothing succeeds.

There are different ways of assassinating a man — by pistol, sword, poison, or moral assassination. They are the same in their results only that the last is the more cruel.

By taking for your justification the pretended principle of general utility you can go to whatever lengths you want.

A lie is useless, since it deceives but once.

Nature in creating certain men designed them for subordinate positions.

Great men are meteors, who, by their burning, light the world.

If aggressors are wrong above, they are right here below.

There are vices and virtues of circumstances.

Since the discovery of printing the intelligent are called on to govern; and those who govern, slave.

He who knows how to flatter also knows how to slander.

The consummate courtier must be one who scorns the object of his flatteries, and is ever ready to destroy him.

There are crises where the good of the nation requires the condemnation of the innocent.

Those who cannot profit by circumstances are ninnies.

The honest are so easy going and rogues so alert, that it is often necessary to employ rogues.

Put a rogue in the limelight and he will act like an honest man.

It is easier to destroy than to restore confidence.

The man fitted for affairs and authority never considers individuals, but things and their consequences.

A congress of the powers is deceit agreed on between diplomats — it is the pen of

Machiavelli combined with the scimitar of Mahomet.

Destiny urges me to a goal of which I am ignorant. Until that goal is attained I am invulnerable, unassailable. When Destiny has accomplished her purpose in me, a fly may suffice to destroy me.

Necessity dominates inclination, will, and right.

The most dangerous counselor is self-love.

To be a successful conqueror one must be cruel.

The strong man is the one who is able to intercept at will the communication between the senses and the mind.

Men who hesitate never succeed in their undertakings.

One never mounts so high as when one does not know how high he is going.

What is begun in feebleness belongs of right to audacity, which makes it legitimately its own by seizing it.

There is nothing so hard to harness as a people which has already shaken off the pack saddle.

The only thing to be done with those one is no longer able to recompense, is to disgrace them.

## II

### PSYCHOLOGY AND MORALS

MEN have their virtues and their vices, their heroisms and their perversities; men are neither wholly good nor wholly bad, but possess and practice all that there is of good and bad here below. Such is the general rule. Temperament, education, the accidents of life, are modifying factors. Outside of this, everything is ordered arrangement, everything is chance. Such has been my rule of expectation and it has usually brought me success.

Man is only a more perfect and better reasoning animal.

Whatever misanthropists may say, ingrates and the perverse are exceptions in the human species.

A philosopher has contended that men are born wicked; it would be a very difficult matter and a useless one to determine by inquiry whether he is right. But this much is certain, the great mass of society are far from being depraved; for if a large majority were criminal or inclined to break the laws, where would the force or power be to prevent or constrain them? And herein is the real blessing of civilization, because this happy result has its origin in her bosom, growing out of her very nature.

Man seldom acts wholly true to his character; he yields to the violence of his feelings, or is carried away by passion.

Our physical qualities are developed by our dangers and our needs.

When small men attempt great enterprises, they always end by reducing them to the level of their mediocrity.

What power there is in imagination — in the imagination of men! The English sailors at St. Helena did not know me, had never seen me, only heard of me, yet what did they not see in me, and what did they not do in my behalf! And the same strange spectacle is repeated in every age, in every country, in every century. Such is fanaticism. Yes, imagination governs the world.

Man loves the marvelous. It has an irresistible charm for him. He is always ready to leave that with which he is familiar to pursue vain inventions.

What are we? What is the future? What is the past? What magic fluid envelops us and hides from us the things it is most important for us to know? We are born, we live, and we die in the midst of the marvelous.

To do all that one is able to do, is to be a man; to do all that one would like to do, would be to be a god.

Man achieves in life only by commanding the capabilities nature has given him, or by creating them within himself by education and by knowing how to profit by the difficulties encountered.

It is said that when we know the type of a man we have the key to his conduct. This is untrue. A thoroughly honest man may do an evil act; or another an unjust act, without being wicked. In such cases the man hardly ever acts in accordance with his type, but from some secret purpose, which up to that moment has been hidden in the deepest recesses of his heart. It is a mistake, too, to say that the face is the mirror of the soul. The truth is, men are very hard to know, and yet, not to be deceived, we must judge them by their present actions, but for the present only.

A mind without memory is a fortress without a garrison.

One is more certain to influence men, to produce more effect on them, by absurdities than by sensible ideas.

It is not true that men never change; they change for the worse, as well as for the better. It is not true they are ungrateful; more often the benefactor rates his favors higher than their worth; and often too he does not allow for circumstances. If few men have the moral force to resist impulses, most men do carry within themselves the germs of virtues as well as of vices, of heroism as well as of cowardice. Such is human nature — education and circumstances do the rest.

Ordinarily men exercise their memory much more than their judgment.

Men are sheep, they always follow the leader.

How many really capable men are children more than once during the day!

When we know our moral weakness we ought to know how to care for our soul as we know how to care for our leg or arm.

I am of the opinion that the good or bad conduct of a child depends entirely on its mother.

There is nothing so imperious as feebleness which feels itself supported by force.

The superior man is not by nature impressionable. We praise him, we blame him; it matters little to him. It is to his own judgment that he listens.

The shortcomings of children are often the result of the bad education they have received from their parents.

One does well only that which one does one's self.

Good sense makes men capable. Self-respect is the breeze which swells the sails and wafts their barks into port.

Death is a dreamless sleep.

True character stands the test of emergencies. Do not be mistaken, it is weakness from which the awakening is rude.

Life is a fleeting dream that loses itself.

Life is strewn with so many dangers, and can be the source of so many misfortunes, that death is not the greatest of them.

How many seemingly impossible things have been accomplished by resolute men because they had to do, or die.

The private life of a man is a light by which one may instructively read.

Men are greedy for emotion; their enthusiasm is his who can cleverly arouse it.

There is no strength without skill.

A man becomes the creature of his uniform.

With audacity one can undertake anything, but not do everything.

Interminable matters are those that present no difficulties.

If success were not a chimera, it would not be so alluring.

The fool has one great advantage over a man of sense — he is always satisfied with himself.

Force is never anything but force, enthusiasm never anything but enthusiasm. But persuasiveness endures and imprints itself on the heart.

We only believe the things we want to believe.

To be believed, make the truth unbelievable.

There are some people who behave decently only toward their enemies.

Simpletons talk of the past, wise men of the present, and fools of the future.

Patriotism is the first of virtues.

The ambition to rule over other minds is the strongest of passions.

Most sentiments are traditions.

The man who practices virtue only in the hope of gaining reputation, is toying with vice.

A man with neither courage nor bravery is a mere thing.

I have no regard for those who affect to despise death; the important thing is to know how to endure the inevitable.

Each hour wasted in youth is a hazard of misfortune taken for the future.

The superior man is undisturbed; praised or blamed, he goes on.

In a narrow sphere great men are blunderers.

Self-interest is the key to commonplace actions.

Severity presumes more faults than it represses.

Strong souls resist pleasures of the senses as mariners shun reefs.

To debate in danger is to hold back in the traces.

Adversity is the midwife of genius.

From wit to good sense is farther than one thinks.

Nothing is more difficult than to decide.

A stroke of fate is like striking a money balance; it indicates a man's real worth.

Nothing that degrades a man is useful for long.

Happiness grows out of circumstances; felicity out of affections.

There is nothing noble that is not great; greatness and immensity make us overlook many defects.

Chance takes account of all our follies.

Judgment matures as well in success as in misfortunes.

Time is a necessary element. When Archimedes offered to raise the world with a lever and fulcrum, he required time. God took seven days to create the universe.

Nothing is so rare as steadfast devotion.

Intelligence precedes force. Force itself is nothing without intelligence. In the heroic age the leader was the strongest man; with civilization he has become the most intelligent of the brave.

In pardoning we rise above those who insult us.

Of what blunders are not the vanity and self love of an ignorant man capable.

The man of projects is always right in drawing-rooms.

No man has friends; it is his good fortune that has.

The fire of youth, the pride of blood, the death of hope, all produce enthusiasts and martyrs and bring forth courageous and desperate decisions.

Temptation reaches the heart through the eye; we are always tempted to yield to what we admire.

It is asked why misfortunes feared often affect us more than those actually experienced. It is because, in imagination as in mathematics, we cannot measure the power of the unknown.

When one has never had reverses, he is due to have them proportionate to his good fortune.

How far short men fall from equaling their pretensions! Do they always know, themselves, what they are?

Genius does not transmit itself from parent to son. There has never been, so far as I know, one single instance in all history of two great poets, two great mathematicians, two great conquerors, two great monarchs, one of whom was a son of the other.

Genius is fire from heaven; but it rarely finds a vessel ready to receive it.

Morality is in itself a complete code.

True happiness, the only true strength, all the consolations of mankind are in religion and morality. Hence all moral religions are beautiful. Aside from dogmas more or less absurd, which, to understand, we must know the people among whom they originated, what is there in the Vedas, the Koran, the old Testament, in Confucius, in them all in a word? a pure morality — that is to say, protection to the weak, respect for the laws of the country, and a belief in one God. But the Gospel alone offers morality freed from absurdities.

One must learn to forgive and not to hold a hostile, bitter attitude of mind, which offends those about us and prevents us from enjoying ourselves; one must recognize human shortcomings and adjust himself to them rather than to be constantly finding fault with them.

It is not necessary to prohibit or encourage oddities of conduct which are not harmful.

I despise ingratitude as the most infamous defect of the heart.

Moralizing is very often only a disguise for slander.

The best way to keep one's word is not to give it.

Wounds given honor never heal; they destroy the moral fiber.

It is not to be disputed that in the marriage relation the oriental family is entirely different from the occidental family. Moral codes therefore are not universal. Man is the minister of Nature, and social relations follow racial differences.

We recognize an honest man by his conduct toward his wife, his family, and his servants.

Has a man the right to kill himself? Yes, if his death will injure no one, and life is a misfortune to him. When is life a misfortune to a man? When it offers him nothing but suffering and sorrow; but as suffering and sorrow change constantly, there is no moment in life when a man has the right to kill himself, except at the moment of his death; since then, only, is the proof forthcoming that his life has been only a web of misfortunes and suffering. The man who, succumbing to the weight of present ills, seeks death, does an injustice to himself, yielding in despair and feebleness to the fantasy of the moment, to which he sacrifices all the possibilities of the future.

There are rogues sufficiently roguish to act like honest men.

Suicide is the act of a gambler who has lost everything, or of a ruined prodigal. It has always been a maxim with me that a man showed more true courage in supporting the ills of life than by ending it.

True heroism consists in rising superior to misfortune.

The Grenadier Gobin committed suicide for love. The circumstances offered a good opportunity. It was the second event of the kind that had happened in the corps within a month. The First Consul directed that there should be included in the orders to the Guard: "That a soldier ought to overcome the melancholy and bitterness of hopeless passion; there is as much true courage in suffering with constancy the despair of the soul, as in standing firm under the fire of a battery; to surrender to disappointment without resisting, to commit suicide to escape from it, is to abandon the field of battle without having gained the victory."

To give suitably is to honor; to give much is to corrupt.

When a man has no courage, he necessarily lacks head, and is unfit to command either himself or others.

The human family has two virtues which we cannot value too highly — courage in man, and modesty in woman.

Let the night dissipate the injuries of the day.

There is no compromise with honor.

So much the worse for those who do not believe in virtue.

## III

### LOVE AND MARRIAGE

FAMILY ties have always seemed to me sacred. I have never been able to believe that we can break them without dishonor, and failing in that which is most sacred to man.

In love the only safety is in flight.

Love is the occupation of the idle, the distraction of the soldier, the danger of the monarch.

Marriage ought not to be permitted between those who have not known each other more than six months.

The civil magistrate who would make impressive the woman's promise of obedience and fidelity, ought to have a formulary. It ought to be emphasized that in leaving the protection of the family the woman passes under that of her husband. Magistrates perform the marriage ceremony without any solemnity. It altogether lacks impressiveness. It should be given a moral quality. Observe the priests; they preach a sermon. Even if it is not heard by the bridal couple wholly occupied with other things, it is by the others present.

Marriage is without doubt the perfect social state.

Love is always the occupation of the idle ranks of society.

In great crises it is the portion of wives to make reverses supportable.

We will hear nothing in derogation of women, we peoples of the occident. We hold them, which is a great mistake, as being almost our own equals. The peoples of the orient are wiser and juster than we. They have declared them the natural property of man. And, in effect, Nature has made them our slaves. It is only because of our foolishness that they have dared to pretend to be our equals. They abuse their privileges in order to corrupt and rule us. For one who inspires us to good, there are a hundred who lead us into folly.

Woman was given to man in order that there might be children. Now one woman alone cannot suffice a man for that purpose; she cannot be his wife while she is nursing; she cannot be his wife while she is sick; she ceases to be his wife when she is no longer able to bear him children. Man, whom Nature has limited neither by age nor by any of these inconveniences, ought therefore to have several wives.

If a man is unfaithful to his wife, confesses it and repents of it, no consequences result. The wife is angry, forgives, is reconciled, sometimes exacting something as the price of reconciliation. It is a different matter if the infidelity is the wife's. She will confess and repent of it in vain, for who will guarantee that no consequences will follow? The injury is irreparable. It cannot be and ought not to be condoned. It is therefore only the failure of judgment, of general recognition and the defect of education, which makes it possible for a woman to believe herself equal in all things to her husband. There is however nothing dishonoring in the difference. Each have their privileges and their obligations. Your privileges, ladies, are beauty, grace, and seductive power; your obligations, dependence and submission.

And moreover of what can you complain after all? Have we not accorded you a soul? You know there are compensations in philosophy. You pretend to equality? But that is foolishness. Woman is our property; we are not hers, for she bears us children but we do not bear her any. She is therefore the man's property as the fruit tree is the gardener's.

A beautiful woman appeals to the eye; a good woman appeals to the heart. One is a jewel, the other a treasure.

The man who allows himself to be governed entirely by his wife is neither himself nor his wife; he is nothing.

I firmly belive that love does more harm than good, and that it would be a blessing from divine providence, if it were banished and men delivered from it.

The most important woman in the world, living or dead, is the one who has borne the most children.

How many men are culpable only because of their weakness for women!

Marriage, to be happy, requires a constant exchange of confidences.

Marriage finds no counterpart in nature.

A woman needs six months of Paris to know what is hers to have, and her realm.

Love is folly committed by two.

Marriage is not always the result of love. Most young people marry in order to secure independence and a position, and take spouses who do not suit them in any way. The law ought to provide a remedy at the moment they realize they have been entirely mistaken. But this indulgence ought to favor neither imprudence nor passion. A woman should be permitted but one divorce, and should not be allowed to remarry for five years afterwards. There should be no divorce after ten years of marriage.

The life filled with love is the guarantee of a happy home. It assures the honor of the wife, and the respect of the husband. It maintains confidence and good relations.

The mental inferiority of women, the instability of their ideas, their destiny in the social order, the necessity of inspiring in them a constant submission, and a soft and complaisant charity — all these make the yoke of religion indispensable.

Women, when they are bad, are worse than men, and more disposed to commit crime. When the sex, which is sweet by inheritance, once becomes degraded, it falls into greater excesses than the other. Women are always either much better or much worse than men.

I do not believe it is in our nature to love impartially. We deceive ourselves when we think we can love two beings, even our own children, equally. There is always a dominant affection.

A man ought never to quarrel with a woman; he should hear her unreason in silence.

## IV

### THINGS POLITICAL

IN politics nothing is immutable. Events carry within them an invincible power. The unwise destroy themselves in resistance. The skillful accept events, take strong hold of them and direct them.

The great difficulty with politics is, that there are no established principles.

If, for the sound and sagacious policies appropriate to a great nation having profound destinies to fulfill, the demagoguery of a party is substituted when powerful enemies confront her, nothing effectual will be accomplished.

The most dangerous power is an abstract sentiment in control of the public authority.

It is only with prudence, sagacity, and much dexterity that great aims are accomplished, and all obstacles surmounted. Otherwise nothing is accomplished.

Power is most dangerous when the public authority is obsessed by an abstract sentiment.

Government is difficult when one is conscientious.

One may lose popularity by a peccadillo as well as by a stroke of statesmanship; when one knows the art of reigning, one stakes his credit only on careful consideration.

What constitutes popularity? Good natured complaisance? Who was more popular, more complaisant than the unfortunate Louis XVI? But what was his fate? He perished! The truth is that one ought to serve his people worthily, and not strive solely to please them. The best way to gain a people is to do that which is best for them. Nothing is more dangerous than to flatter a people. If it does not get what it wants immediately, it is irritated and thinks that promises have not been kept; and if then it is resisted, it hates so much the more as it feels itself deceived.

One does not govern a nation by half-measures. In all public acts force, order, and consistency are necessary.

The duties of the head of the nation are not those of the people. The duty of the people is to obey the laws.

The thing to avoid is not so much error as self-contradiction. It is especially by the latter that authority loses its force.

Lead the ideas of your time and they will accompany and support you; fall behind them and they drag you along with them; oppose them and they will overwhelm you.

There is no such thing as an absolute despotism; it is only relative. A man cannot wholly free himself from obligation to his fellows. A sultan who cut off heads from caprice, would quickly lose his own in the same way. Excesses tend to check themselves by reason of their own violence. What the ocean gains in one place it loses in another.

We are made weak both by idleness and distrust of ourselves. Unfortunate, indeed, is he who suffers from both. If he is a mere individual he becomes nothing; if he is a king he is lost.

A prince should suspect everything.

In politics, an absurdity is not an impediment.

One who wants to be a force in government must be ready to put himself in peril; if need be, to dare assassination.

Government must be administered for the general good without worrying about whether it pleases this or that individual. If one attempts a middle course, serving each party, he attempts an absurd equilibrium, arouses dissatisfaction in the great majority where good sense is always found; for it is the acquiescence of the great body of the people that makes public opinion sovereign.

Public opinion is the thermometer a monarch should constantly consult.

It must not be forgotten that rigorous authority and justice are the kindness of kings. The kindness of kings and that of individuals are not to be confounded.

I do not allow myself to be imposed upon by reputations. Former services I consider only a school in which one ought to have learned to serve better. Within a short time I have become an old administrator. The most difficult art is not in the choice of men, but in giving to the men chosen the highest service of which they are capable.

The great orators who sway assemblies by the brilliancy of their speech, are in general very ordinary statesmen. It is useless to contend with them by words; they will always have more sonorous phrases than yours. The thing to do is to meet their glibness with precise, logical reasoning.

Their strength is in vagueness. One must pin them down to facts. This method is death to their pretensions.

Immorality is, without possibility of contradiction, the worst thing that can be found in a sovereign, for the reason that it at once makes immorality fashionable. It is emulated as a point of honor. It fortifies all vices, strikes at all virtue, infects society with a veritable plague. It is the scourge of a nation.

I would conceive a bad opinion of a government all of whose edicts were drafted in a literary style. The true art is that each edict have the style and character of the class it affects.

Wherever there is a source of incontestable power, men will be found to draw it to themselves.

France is the country where officials have the least influence. To rely on them is to build on sand. Great things are done in France only by relying on the people. Moreover a government ought to seek its support from that very source.

Posterity alone rightly judges kings. Posterity alone has the right to accord or withhold honors.

Democracy exalts sovereignty; but aristocracy alone maintains it.

The trade of being a king is not child's play in this century. It is inevitable that the manners of kings should change with the manners of the people. In order to have the right to the services of the people, it is necessary to begin by serving them well.

We must distinguish between the acts of a sovereign, as such, and those of an individual who is unconstrained as to his opinions. State policy permits, and even requires, in the one, what should be without excuse in the other.

A government in appealing to the intelligence of all its citizens, acts in its own interest and strengthens the social edifice;

every citizen ought to be interested in the security of the state.

A throne is only a bench covered with velvet.

Obedience to public authority ought not to be based either on ignorance or stupidity.

No constitution continues unchanged; the change it undergoes depends on men and circumstances. If there are objections to an overstrong government, there are still more to a weak one. Every day it is constrained to violate positive laws; there is no other way to do. Without doing it, it is impossible to get along.

I had Baumont and two hundred others in the west arrested as grain smugglers. There was not a single minister who might not have been accused. The government could not be arbitrary, because it did not have the support of a feudal system, a class financially interested in it, nor prejudices. The day the government should become arbitrary it would lose the support of public opinion and would be lost. There was need of an extraordinary council for these unforeseen cases. The senate served very well.

I complained of wrongs done a Frenchman at Venice, and demanded reparation. They urged the laws as a difficulty in the way. I threatened to destroy them and pointed out that they had the Council of Ten and the Judges of the Inquisition, etc. The Judges of the Inquisition easily found a way to meet my demands.

The true policy of a government is to make use of aristocracy, but under the forms and in the spirit of democracy.

A form of government which is not the result of a long series of emergencies, of misfortunes, and of efforts and attempts on the part of a people, will never take very deep root.

A prince should never allow the spirit of intrigue and faction to triumph over his authority, or a mean spirit of unsteadiness and opposition to discredit that fundamental sovereignty which is the foundation of social order and the true source of all that benefits a people.

The old patched monarchies will last only as long as the people do not realize their own power. Such structures always perish through their foundations.

Legislation is a weapon that a government ought always to use when national prosperity is in danger.

The men who have changed the universe have never accomplished it by changing officials but always by inspiring the people.

Prudence is good when one has the choice of means. When one hasn't, it is daring which achieves success.

Republics are not to be made from old monarchies.

In revolutions everything is speedily forgotten. The good that you do today will be forgotten tomorrow. Conditions once changed, gratitude, friendship, relationship — all ties are broken, and each person seeks his own interest.

In national crises, the reasonable man is the one who is considered feeble, because passion resembles force.

A man at the head of a struggling party in civil turmoil is called a rebel chief. But when he has succeeded, when he has done great deeds, and established his country and himself, he is given the name of general, and sovereign, and that sort of thing. It is success that gives him the title. If he had been unfortunate he would have continued to be a rebel chief, and perhaps have perished on the scaffold. It is success which makes men great.

Anarchy invariably leads to arbitrary government.

Provisional governments placed in difficult circumstances ought to concern themselves exclusively with the public safety and the interests of the country.

It is inevitable that a government which follows the storms of revolution and which is menaced by enemies from without and disturbed by intrigue within, will be somewhat harsh.

Insurrection and the emigration of the nobility are diseases of the skin. Terrorism is an internal disease.

In revolutions, like attracts like, as it does in the physical world.

A universal rule: Never a revolution without terror.

Among nations and in revolutions, aristocracy always exists. If you attempt to get rid of it by destroying the nobility, it immediately re-establishes itself among the rich and powerful families of the third estate. Destroy it there, and it survives and takes refuge among the leaders of workmen and of the people. A prince gains nothing by this shifting of aristocracy. On the contrary he re-establishes stable conditions by permitting it to continue as it is, readjusting, however, the old order to the new principles.

With good fortune one renders a people glorious; it requires much firmness to make them happy.

Sooner or later the public interests overcome minor prejudices.

In order that a people may be free, it is necessary that the governed be sages, and those who govern, gods.

Incidents should not govern state policies; but state policies, incidents.

Neutrality consists in having equal weights and measures for each. In statecraft it is nonsense, for our interest always lies with the triumph of one or the other.

Constitutions are good only as we make progress under them.

The policy which is not moral must glorify morality.

Display is to power what ceremony is to religion.

Commerce unites men. Whatever unites men leads them to act together. Commerce is therefore essentially dangerous to arbitrary authority.

One may risk a coup d'état to gain power, but never to strengthen it; for in that case the supreme authority is attacked.

The laws of circumstance are abolished by new circumstances.

A good philosopher makes a bad citizen.

A man will fight harder for his interests than for his rights.

To win confidence in advance of success, is the most difficult political accomplishment.

When deplorable weakness and indecision manifest themselves in the counsels of power; when, yielding in turn to the influence of opposing parties, and living from day to day without fixed plans or a determined policy, it has shown the completeness of its incapacity, and when the most moderate citizens are forced to admit that the state is no longer governed; when, in fact, to its incompetency the administration suffers, what in the eyes of a proud people is the greatest humiliation possible, I mean to say the contempt of foreign nations, then a vague inquietude spreads throughout the community, concern for national preservation arises, and, turning its gaze on itself, it seems to search for a man able to save it.

Such a tutelary genius *(See Note 2)* every numerous nation contains within itself, though sometimes he is slow in appearing. In truth, it is not sufficient that he exists, he must be known — he must know himself. Until then all efforts are vain, all expedients fail. The mere inertia of the majority saves the phantom government, and, in spite of its incapacity and weakness, the efforts of its enemies do not prevail against it. But let this liberator, impatiently awaited, suddenly give a sign of his existence, the national instinct at once divines him and calls him. Obstacles vanish before him, and the whole nation, as by a common impulse, following in his train seems to say: There is the man!

If obedience is the result of the instinct of the masses, revolt is the result of their thought.

The people are capable of good judgment when they do not listen to demagogues. Ranters never help matters any, and always make them worse.

In revolutions there are only two sorts of men, those who cause them and those who profit by them.

Thrones are never repaired.

A revolution is an opinion which utilizes bayonets.

Some revolutions are inevitable. There are moral eruptions, just as the outbreak of volcanoes are physical eruptions. When the chemical combinations which produce them are complete, the volcanic eruptions burst forth, just as revolutions do when the moral factors are in the right state. In order to foresee them the trend of ideas must be understandingly observed.

A revolution is a vicious circle — it is caused by excesses and it brings them.

Young men accomplish revolutions which older men have prepared.

Once committed to a course, a people is not to be stopped.

There is room for neither passion nor prejudice in public affairs; the only permissible passion is that for the public welfare.

Charles the First perished because he resisted, Louis XVI because he did not. Neither comprehended the strength of inertia which is the secret of great reigns.

In statesmanship there are predicaments from which it is impossible to escape without some wrongdoing.

One can lead a nation only by helping it see a bright outlook. A leader is a dealer in hope.

It is rare that a legislature reasons. It is too quickly impassioned.

Large legislative bodies resolve themselves into coteries, and coteries into jealousies.

Nations must be saved in spite of themselves.

Parties weaken themselves by their fear of capable men.

A political faction never tolerates a permanent leader. It needs one for each passion.

During the Revolution the French were never without a king.

The hereditary character of orders of nobility deprives both noble and commoner of the spirit of emulation.

Necessity can be overcome only by absolute power.

A revolution is effected when it is only necessary to get rid of one man.

Absolute power represses ambitions and makes selection; democracy unchains all without examination.

A usurper has had too many masters not to begin by being arbitrary.

Nothing should resemble a man less than a king.

I will be the Brutus of kings and the Caesar of the republic.

Discipline is permanent only as it is appropriate to the character of the nation.

Never have national assemblies combined prudence and energy, wisdom and vigor.

Under a system of absolute government, only one will is necessary to destroy an abuse; under a representative system, five hundred are necessary.

The people never choose real legislators.

In spite of all their horrors, revolutions are nevertheless the true cause of regeneration in public customs.

Democracy may become frenzied, but it has feelings and can be moved. As for aristocracy, it is always cold and never forgives.

I have a very poor opinion of a government which lacks the power to interdict the things that are capable of causing friction with foreign governments.

I espouse no party but the masses. My policy is to complete the fusion of the whole people.

The institution of a national nobility is not contrary to equality. It is necessary to maintain the social order. No social order has ever been established on agrarian laws. The principle of private property and of transmission by contract of sale, by gift during life, or by will, is a fundamental principle which does not detract from equality. From this principle is derived the custom of transmitting from father to son the remembrance of services rendered to the state. Fortunes are sometimes acquired by means shameful or criminal. Titles acquired by services to the state rise from a pure and honorable source. Their transmission to posterity is only simple justice *(See Note 3).*

I must govern all without regard to what each has done. They have rallied to me to enjoy security. They would abandon me tomorrow if matters became problematical.

The laws of most countries are made to oppress the unfortunate and to protect the powerful.

We frustrate many designs against us by pretending not to see them.

Those who avenge on principle are ferocious and implacable.

The name and the power of government signify nothing, provided citizens are equal in their rights, and that justice is well administered.

There are only two classes in Europe, those who want privileges, and those who spurn them.

The man the least free is the man bound to party.

Nothing goes well in a political system where words play with things.

Social law is able to give all men the same rights, though nature will never give them equal abilities.

Prosperity is the best tie between prince and people.

Government ought to be a continuous demonstration.

The susceptibility of a government is its own accusation of weakness.

All governments ought to see men only in mass.

It is the unity of interests which makes the strength of governments.

Absolute power must be essentially paternal; otherwise it will be overthrown.

Every man who is worth thirty millions and is not wedded to them, is dangerous to the government.

In the last analysis there must be a military quality in government. One governs a horse only with boots and spurs.

The foundation of all authority is in the advantage of those who obey.

The wars of the Revolution have ennobled the entire French nation.

Appealing to foreigners is a criminal act.

A party which sustains itself only by foreign bayonets is vanquished.

The old nobility would have continued to exist if it had not been more concerned with branches than with roots.

Out of a hundred favorites of kings, ninety-five have been hanged.

The court, taken collectively, exercises no direct influence on the tone and the manners of a nation. It affects these only because its elements, those who compose it, spread, each in his own sphere of activity, that which they have drawn from the common source. The tone of the court, therefore, affects the whole nation only by spreading through the various ranks of society.

It is a great mistake of the court not to give itself leadership.

The old nobility would have survived if it had known enough to become master of writing materials.

A prince who is afraid is liable to be overthrown at any moment.

To listen to the interests of all, marks an ordinary government; to foresee them, marks a great government.

A sovereign ought to occupy himself with seeking the good that is in the bad, and conversely.

A government can live only in accordance with its own principles.

The wisdom of the chief of the state is to foresee events. At the very moment when he is the most beneficent he is accused of tyranny.

It is not necessary that the chief of the state should be the chief of a party.

The eminence of sovereigns depends on that of their peoples.

A great monarch is the one who foresees results at all times.

Palace troops are dangerous in proportion as the sovereign is absolute.

It is good policy to make a people believe they are free. It is good government to make them as happy as they wish to be.

The chief of state ought no more to abandon the government of ideas than the government of men.

The expression "political virtue," is nonsense.

Peace is the first of needs, as it is the first of glories.

Peace ought to be the result of a system well considered, founded on the true interests of the different countries, honorable to each, and ought not to be either a capitulation or the result of a threat.

A sovereign who attaches himself to a faction unsteadies his bark and hastens shipwreck.

The chief of state must cooperate even with the bad for the triumph of public affairs.

A sovereign ought not to rely either on word or look.

The conspirators who unite to shake off a tyranny, commence by submitting to that of a chief.

Imagination has done more harm than facts. It is the capital enemy of monarchs.

Honors are, for a sovereign, a moral treasury.

It is by wounding the self-love of princes that we influence their deliberations.

A material conspiracy is ended the moment we seize the hand which holds the dagger; a moral conspiracy never ends.

A state is better off with ministers of moderate ability who continue in office, than with able ones when changes are frequent.

Indecision in fundamental things is to government what paralysis is to the movements of the limbs.

Etiquette is the prison of kings.

Public opinion is a mysterious, invisible power, which nothing can resist. Nothing is more changeable, more intangible, or stronger. And yet, capricious as it is, it is, nevertheless, right, reasonable, and just, much oftener than we are disposed to think it is.

It is seldom that men of moderate ability, when in authority, have honest purposes; they always make a mess of things.

Emergency legislation is itself an indictment of the power that enacts it.

One can escape the arbitrariness of judges only by placing one's self under the despotism of law.

The most deceptive policy is playing one faction against another, and flattering yourself that you dominate both.

In my present situation (1814), I find nobility only in the rabble which I have neglected, and rabble only in the nobility I have created.

Compromises weaken power.

In all public acts there should be strength, perseverance, and singleness.

When, among a people, all want place, one finds himself sold out in advance.

The advent of cannon killed the feudal system; ink will kill the modern social organization.

I will respect the conclusions of public opinion when they are legitimate; but public opinion has caprices one must scorn.

In a government, it is not the inconsequential who need watching, it is the strong. It is to the latter that it is necessary to direct constant attention. Loosen the rein on the great and at once they encroach on the sovereign. Why occupy one's self so much with the rich? The rich have all the advantages that organized society gives.

Their very wealth protects them far too well. The strength, the future of a government, the power of a throne, are in the common people, and the dangers which menace it are in the strong. Sovereigns, protect the common people if you wish that in their turn they should protect you.

Absolute power has no need to lie; it acts, and says nothing. A responsible government is always obliged to speak, and is led into ignoble lies. In a short time it becomes discredited and falls, scorned. Absolute power at least falls hated.

Political laws compared with those of humanity have brief duration. They grow out of conditions and manners, and as conditions and manners change, they change with them.

I have sown liberty with a bountiful hand wherever I have established my Civil Code *(See Note 4)*.

In all civilized countries, mere strength yields to civil requirements. Bayonets bow down before the priest who speaks in the name of heaven, and before the man who inspires respect by his knowledge.

There are more chances of securing a good sovereign by heredity than by election.

Such is the inevitable trend of these numerous bodies (the Chambers); they perish for lack of harmony. Leaders are as necessary to them as to armies. In the latter they are appointed. But men of great talent, the superior geniuses, make themselves masters of assemblies and of governments.

The Revolution ought to teach that nothing is foreseen.

The great powers suffer from indigestion.

A king must not allow himself to be crushed by misfortune.

## V

### CONCERNING THE FINE ARTS

I LOOK on scholars and wits as I do on coquettes. It is all right to call on either, to chat with them, but not to take a coquette for a wife, or the others for ministers.

Great writers are but esteemed drivelers.

A stupid is only a bore; a pedant is unbearable.

If the French language has become a universal language, it is to the genius of men of letters that we owe it.

The French language is the most cultivated modern language, and it is not necessary to go to any other for inscriptions for monuments.

The French language is not a perfect language. It lacks many words. It imperfectly expresses a crowd of things — a sound impression, a great thought. It is rather the language of wit than of genius.

The classics are written by rhetoricians, while they ought to be written only by statesmen, or men of the world.

A book in which there were no lies would be a curiosity.

Books are too argumentative not to corrupt a nation by dishabituating it from fact.

The only encouragement for poets are the places in the Institute, because these give to them a standing in the nation.

The art of the sovereign, like that of the minister, is to give refulgence to good works.

There ought to be power to give pensions to men of letters. To those who are in need, the Minister of Interior gives 200,000 francs per annum, by way of relief. It is a disagreeable form of disbursing it, and has nothing in keeping with the national source from which it comes. It is charity.

All men of genius, and all those who have gained rank in the republic of letters, are brothers, whatever may be the land of their nativity.

Newspapers are not history, any more than bulletins are.

Historians too often make history unintelligible by their ignorance, or by their laziness. When they do not understand, or do not know, they draw on their imagination, instead of making researches which would lead them to the truth.

History, as I take it, ought to present individuals or peoples just as they have shown themselves to be at the height of their accomplishment. Account must be taken of the external circumstances, which must necessarily exert a great influence on their actions; and a clear view must be had of the limits within which this influence was exercised. The Roman Emperors were not as bad as Tacitus painted them. Moreover, I much prefer Montesquieu to Tacitus. He is juster, and his criticism is more conformable to truth.

It must be recognized that the real truths of history are hard to discover. Happily, for the most part, they are rather matters of curiosity than of real importance. There are so many verities! This historical verity so much appealed to, which each zealously invokes, is too often only a word. Truth is impossible at the moment of events, in the heat of aroused passions; if, later, accord is restored, only those interested remain; there are none to controvert. But what really is this historical verity in most cases? a lie agreed on, as some one has very wittily said. In every matter there are two very distinct elements — the actual facts, and the motives behind them. The actual facts, it would seem, ought to be incontrovertible; and yet, there are some which remain eternally in dispute. As to motives, what are the means of discovering them, even assuming the good faith of the narrators? And what will they be if the narrators are actuated by bad faith, by interest and passion? I have given an order, but who is able to read my innermost thought, my real intention? Yet, nevertheless, each will take this order, measure it with his own yardstick, adjust it to his own theories, his individual beliefs. And each will hold firmly to what he relates. And the lesser writers who take it from these privileged lips will be as sure of it in their turn! And then the memoirs and the diaries and the drawing-room anecdotes and witty speeches which follow in their train! That nevertheless is history.

Little love scenes in tragedy are banal; our age is advancing, and everything must advance with it.

History proves that detraction falls quickly into contempt. If detractors could only look through the mass of rubbish there is in the National Library that has been written against Henry IV and Louis XIV, they would be humiliated by their impotence; they have not left an impression.

Verse is only the embroidery of the dramatic fabric.

A good tragedy always grows better every day. High tragedy is the school of great men. It is the duty of sovereigns to encourage and promote it. It is not necessary to be a poet to judge it. It is sufficient to know men and things, to have elevation of mind, a statesmanlike outlook.

France owes to Corneille some of her finest achievements. If he were alive, I would make him a prince.

I love high tragedy; the sublime, like that of Corneille. In tragedy great men are more truly great than in history. We see them only in the crises which unfold them, in the moments of supreme decision; and we are not burdened with all the preparatory details and conjectures, often false, which the historian gives us. There is equal gain for glory, for there is enough weakness, uncertainty, and doubt in men; but there ought to be none in heroes. Tragedy should be an heroic statue in which nothing of the weakness or quivering of the flesh is seen. It should be the "Perseus" of Benvenuto Cellini, that group sublime and true which owes its very existence (though its appearance gives no hint of it) to the pewter plates and dishes which the artist in the fury of desperation flung into his seething crucible to give his bronze the fit quality for his masterpiece.

I am thankful that tragedy has thus magnified some men, or rather has given them the true stature of superior men in a mortal body. I have often wished that our poets had been able to do that for our modern heroes. And why not? Genius has not grown less since the time of Caesar. But our poets have known nothing of modern genius, not more of Henry IV than of Philip the Fair *(See Note 5).*

Tragedy should be the school of kings and of nations. It forms the highest pinnacle to which poets can attain.

Melodramas are the tragedies of chambermaids.

In the *Agamemnon* of Aeschylus, what I admire is the great strength joined to great simplicity which is exhibited. I am struck, more than by anything else, by the gradations of terror which characterize the productions of this father of tragedy. And there is there, moreover, the first spark from which has been kindled our beautiful modern flame.

It is not fair to paint everything black, as Tacitus does. He has not sufficiently sought out the causes, and the interior springs, of events; he has not sufficiently studied the mystery of facts and of motives. He has not sufficiently sought for and scrutinized their interplay, to transmit a just and impartial judgment to posterity.

Dante is to me the greatest genius of modern times. Dante is a sun who shines in all his brilliancy in the midst of profound night. Everything in him is extraordinary. His originality, especially, assigns to him a rank apart. Ariosto has imitated the romance of chivalry, and the poems of the ancients. Tasso has done the same thing.

Dante has not deigned to take his inspiration from any other. He has wished to be himself, himself alone; in a word, to create. He has occupied a vast space, and has filled it with the superiority of a sublime mind. He is diverse, strong, and gracious. He has imagination, warmth, and enthusiasm. He makes his reader tremble, shed tears, feel the thrill of honor in a way that is the height of art. Severe and menacing, he has terrible imprecations for crime, scourgings for vice, sorrow for misfortune. As a citizen, affected by the laws of the republic, he thunders against its oppressors, but he is always ready to excuse his native city. Florence is ever to him his sweet, beloved country, dear to his heart. I am envious for my dear France, that she has never produced a rival to Dante; that this Colossus has not had his equal among us. No, there is no reputation which can be compared to his.

It is astonishing how poorly Voltaire bears reading *(See Note 6)*. When the pomp and diction, the influence of the situation, no longer mislead analysis or good taste, then he loses a thousand per cent at once.

Homer was the encyclopedist of his epoch *(See Note 7)*.

A prelate like Fenelon *(See Note 8)*, is the finest gift heaven can bestow on a great city, and a government.

I disapprove of giving La Fontaine to children not old enough to understand him *(See Note 9)*. There is too much irony in the fable of the wolf and the lamb to bring it within the reach of children. It errs, moreover, to my mind in its purpose and its trend. It is not true that the right of the stronger is the better. And if it seems to be, that is the wrong, the abuse, that ought to be condemned. The wolf, therefore, ought to have choked himself in eating the lamb.

Well done as Racine's *(See Note 10)* masterpieces are in themselves, he has, nevertheless, flavored them with a perpetual gallantry, an eternal love, with his tone of insipid sweetness, his tiresome surroundings. But still it is not wholly his fault; it was the vice and the manners of his time. Love then, and later still, was the principal affair of life with everyone. It always is in the idle strata of society. As for us, we in our generation have been rudely distracted from it by the Revolution and its stirring effects.

Without question, *Tartuffe (See Note 11)* in its entirety, is from a master hand. It is the masterpiece of an inimitable man. Nevertheless, this play is of such a character that for my part I do not hesitate to say that if it had been written in my time I would not have permitted it to be presented.

*Gil Blas* is witty *(See Note 12)*, but he deserved the galleys, he and all of his.

*The Genius of Christianity*, by De Chateaubriand *(See Note 13)*, is a work of lead and gold, but the gold predominates.

La Harpe *(See Note 14)* was a man without genius, without imagination, freezingly cold to his neighbors. He was later a rabid devotee without being more sincere. He conspired against the state through pride.

Everything that is great and national in character ought to acknowledge the genius of De Chateaubriand.

I read a few chapters of Madame de Stael's *(See Note 15) Corinne,* but I couldn't finish it. Madame de Stael has drawn herself so well in her heroine, that she has succeeded in making me cordially hate her. I see her, I hear her, I feel her, I want to get away from her, and I throw down the book.

The home of Madame de Stael at Coppet became a veritable arsenal against me. Thither came many to be armed as knights against me. She occupied herself in stirring up enemies against me, and fought me herself. She was at the same time Armide and Clorinde *(See Note 16).* And yet, after all, it is only true to say that no one can deny that Madame de Stael is a woman of very great talent, greatly distinguished, and of much strength of character. She will endure.

Beaumarchais *(See Note 17)* was a man without morals, without principle, a dealer in literature, rather than a man of letters; aspiring to fortune and finding every means good by which he could reach it; endowed with a keen mind, observant, mocking, and satirical; carrying audacity to effrontery; insolent with the great, eating from their hand; armored against all infamies, and sacrificing everything to his insatiable desire to be the most talked of man in Paris. Under my reign such a man would have been locked up as a madman. It would have been called arbitrary, but what a service it would have been to society.

The Theatre Française *(See Note 18)* ought to be supported because it is a part of the national glory. But it ought to reduce the price of seats in the parquette, to twenty sous on Sunday, in order that the people may be able to enjoy it. We do not have to do things always just as they have been done in the past, as if it were impossible to do better.

The division of labor, which has brought such perfection in mechanical industries, is altogether fatal when applied to productions of the mind. All work of the mind is superior in proportion as the mind that produces it is universal.

It is scarcely to be believed, yet at the time of the Revolution Voltaire had dethroned Corneille and Racine. We were asleep to the beauties of these; it was the First Consul who brought about the awakening.

You can't do anything with a philosopher.

It has been the desire of my heart to see the artists of France surpass the glory of Athens and of Italy.

The Arcs de Triomphe would be futile work, serving no purpose, and I would not have built them if I had not thought them a means of encouraging architecture. I hoped with the Arcs de Triomphe to nourish the architecture of France for twenty years.

In science the world of details is yet to be discovered.

Opera costs the government eight hundred thousand francs a year; it is necessary to sustain an establishment which flatters the national vanity. Grand Opera alone should be permitted to produce ballets.

Why did not the Revolution, which destroyed so much, demolish the Chateau of Versailles? I would not have a fort of Louis XIV on my hands, and to tolerate an old, badly built chateau, is to make of it, as one has said, " a favorite without merit " *(See Note 19)*.

## VI

### ADMINISTRATION

THERE ought to be authority to give pensions to men who have rendered service as civil functionaries, such as prefects, superior judges, counsellors of state, and to their widows. When there is no future for public functionaries, they abuse their places. The Directory, unable to give pensions, gave a pecuniary interest in official business, something very reprehensible.

A French functionary ought to excite envy always, never pity.

More character is required in administration than in war.

The thing is, not to select the man whom the place fits, but the man who fits the place.

Great functionaries, however economical and even parsimonious they may be in their private life, should be generous and free-handed in their public life.

The emoluments of public employes ought to be such as to permit a style of living corresponding to the importance of their functions. The French ought to maintain in everything an attitude befitting the representatives of the greatest nation in the world.

Laws which are consistent in theory often prove chaotic in practice.

In practical administration, experience is everything.

The prefects *(See Note 20)*, with all the authority and the local resources with which they found themselves invested, were emperors on a small scale. And as their whole power came from the appointing power, of which they were but the instruments, as all the influence they had arose from their immediate employment, and none of it from their own individuality, and as they owned none of the soil they ruled, they had all the advantages of the old despotic functionaries, without any of their disadvantages. It had been absolutely necessary to give this extensive power. I found myself dictator; circumstances had willed it thus. It was therefore necessary that the system centering in me, should be in perfect harmony with my will; otherwise there was danger of it breaking down. The governmental network with which I covered the country, necessitated keen tension, and perfect elasticity, if we were to repel promptly and effectively the terrific blows constantly aimed at us.

There must of necessity be some intermediary means between the people and the executive power, otherwise nothing will be accomplished.

There is too much centralization of power in France. I wish there were less authority in Paris, and more in each locality.

Without system and method, administration becomes chaos, and there is neither public finances nor public credit; and private fortunes collapse with the collapse of the state.

France abounds in practical, capable men; the thing is to find them, and to give them the means of proving themselves. There are men at the plow who ought to be in the Council of State; and ministers of state who ought to be at the plow.

I wish there were a teaching body which should be a nursery of teachers, school principals, and schoolmasters, and would arouse in them a splendid spirit of emulation. Young men who devote themselves to teaching ought to have the prospect of rising from one grade to another to the highest places in the state. The feet of this great teaching body should be in the schools, and its head in the Senate. But the principle of celibacy is necessary, to this extent, that schoolmasters ought not to be allowed to marry until they are twenty-five or thirty years of age, and have reached a salary of three or four thousand francs a year, and have made sufficient economies. This is, after all, only the application of the customary foresight as to marriage in all ranks of society.

I am conscious that in the matter of the instruction of youth, the Jesuits have left a very great void. I have no wish to reestablish them, or any other body subject to alien control. But I do believe myself under obligations to organize a system of education for the rising generation in such a way that oversight of its political and moral opinions may be secured.

I believe also that it is wise in this organization to require celibacy up to a certain age; not absolute celibacy, for, without contradiction, marriage is the perfect social state.

This teaching body should be so constituted that records will be kept of each child above nine years of age.

The Frenchman is so inclined to be infatuated with the foreigner that it is, perhaps, not necessary to teach pupils foreign languages. One of the obstacles to the re-establishment of our marine is the high opinion that our sailors have of the superiority of the English. It was Prusso-mania which lost the battle of Rossbach *(See Note 21)*.

There will never be a fixed policy of state until there is a teaching body with fixed principles. As long as no one is taught from childhood that it is necessary to be a republican or a monarchist, Catholic or without religion, the state will never form a nation. It will rest on uncertain and unstable foundations. It will be constantly subject to disorders and changes.

It is affirmed that the schools maintained by the lay Brothers are likely to introduce in the University a dangerous element, and it is proposed to exclude them from its jurisdiction. I cannot understand the species of fanaticism with which some persons are animated against the lay Brothers. It is purely a prejudice. Moreover, those who propose to leave the Brothers outside the University do not realize that they are going counter to their own purposes. It is by including them in the University that they will become a part of the civil order, and the danger of their independence will be forestalled. They will not be dangerous when they no longer have a foreign or an unknown head *(See Note 22)*.

There is no necessity for granting too easily the degree of Doctor of the University. The postulant ought to be examined on matters more difficult; for example, on the comparison of languages. There would be nothing out of the way in requiring a candidate to speak in Latin for an hour and a half. It is not necessary that everybody should become a doctor.

I have never intended that professors should undertake the establishment of colleges on their own account. That would be ridiculous. On the other hand, I have never wanted their stipends to be fixed independently of the number of students. I have believed their stipends should be in proportion to the increase in the number of students, so that they would have an interest in the success of these establishments. Moreover, it is not possible to have a uniform scale of stipends. They must be graded according to locality and merit.

There are some changes to be made in the authority regarding publications which it is proposed to give the University. It is not necessary that it should arrogate any power to itself to repress works which are published by others. Its rights should be limited to replying to them, to putting them on the expurgatory index of the University, and to punishing professors who avail themselves of such works in their teaching. These means will be sufficient to prevent youth from being carried away by the thousand jarring errors that assail them, or being drawn into scientific or literary heresies.

The religious orders would be the best teaching bodies if they could renounce their allegiance to a foreign head.

The project of a school of arts and crafts for the children of soldiers and sailors, has been considered for the purpose of giving them an education suitable to their station. It may be said that it would be better to apprentice them to masters. But that would answer only for a year or two, and would fail very soon. There is, moreover, a political purpose. It is important. There should be a bringing together of all classes, and in a national spirit. We have already followed this system for the middle classes. The Lycees *(See Note 23)* should supply lawyers, doctors, and educated soldiers. In order to extend this to the lower classes two other schools should be established, and in them should be placed the children of the newly annexed departments in order that they may be taught French. It is from among these that we will one day take the workmen for our ports for our military workshops and for our colonies.

The law looks on the Commissioners of War as civil agents only, while more courage and military skill are required of them than even of military officers. The courage required is essentially moral. It is never the result of anything but association with danger. . . . One is revolted in hearing daily individuals of different bureaus admit, and even almost glory in, having had fear.

Our system of finance should consist in the creation of a great number of indirect contributions, of which the very moderate rate would be capable of being increased to the measure of need.

It seems that the price of stocks, in Paris, is everybody's business except that of the real owners. The so-called buyers and sellers do nothing, in fact, but make bets with one another that such will be at such a time the state of the market. Each of them, in order to make a living, tries to direct the policies of the whole of Europe toward the end he desires. Each invents, comments on, or misrepresents the facts, penetrates the councils and the cabinets of ministers, the secrets of courts; makes ambassadors speak; decides peace and war; stirs up and misleads opinion, always so avid of novelties and of errors, especially in France, that the more one misleads it the more empire he has over it. And this scandalous influence is not alone exercised by that crowd of adventurers called stock-jobbers. The stock-brokers themselves, to whom all personal speculation is interdicted by the nature of their business, take advantage of their position and buy and sell on their own account. Often they become opposed in interest to those, even, whom they call their clients. Public morals alone would require the suppression of this abuse, and still other motives join with this. The rights of liberty end where abuses commence.

I do not want to have the appearance of presenting a law for the reestablishment of the salt tax *(See Note 24)*. It is not that I would fear to reestablish it if I thought it useful to the nation; but if I did, I would do it openly and above board. I am sometimes a fox, but I know how to be a lion.

Commerce is only possible by reason of confidence. There can be no confidence under a feeble government. There is no confidence in a country rent by factions.

Commerce is an honorable calling, but its essential base must be prudence and economy. The merchant must not gain his fortune as one gains a battle; he should make little, but constantly.

I want to do what is best for my people, and I will not be deterred by the murmurs of the taxpayers. France needs large revenues. They will be secured. I want to establish and systematize for my successors such resources as will supply them with the extraordinary means which I have been able to create.

Why is there no public spirit in France? It is because the land owner is obliged to make his court to the administration. If he is not in its favor, he can be ruined. Decisions in land title cases are arbitrary. It is from this that in no other nation is there such servile attachment to the government as in France, because only there is title to land dependent on the government. Nothing has ever been done for land titles in France. Whoever shall frame a good registration law will merit a statue.

Finances founded on good agriculture will never be ruined.

I would find it very useful to be able to refer to the Council of State the abuses committed by the prefects. The fear of this would restrain the few who give me cause of complaint.

There is no need of any alliance between the Bank and the Treasury. Often a trifling transfer of funds would carry with it secrets of state.

Courts of Special Instance (Special Courts) cannot be dangerous when the Supreme Court passes on their competency.

It is easy to determine with precision misdemeanors which will come within the jurisdiction of these courts. I wish they could have jurisdiction in cases of attempts against the police, the crimes of second offenders, runaways from the galleys, and also crimes committed by malefactors operating together. Simple individuals, like jurors, are intimidated by the sight of a band of culpables. It has been thought, and rightly, that experienced judges would not be as susceptible to these impressions of fear. That is the true and only reason for establishing these courts of Special Instance.

Care must be taken not to give the Court of Appeals such powers as will, insensibly, lead it to go into questions of fact.

Do not imagine that the power to pardon can be exercised with impunity, or that society will applaud every use of it by the monarch. Society will disapprove when it is extended to felons, to murderers, because then it becomes dangerous to the social order.

It is in sentences for violation of fiscal regulations, and, more particularly still, in those for political delinquencies, that clemency is well placed. In these matters the theory is that it is the sovereign who has been attacked, and therefore there is a certain nobility in pardon. At the first reports of an offense of this kind, the interested public ranges itself on the side of the culprit, and not on that of the punishing power. If the prince remits the punishment, the people think of him as superior to the offense, and opinion is turned against the offender. If the prince follows the opposite course, he gains the reputation of being hateful, and tyrannical. If he extends pardon in the case of odious crimes, he gains the reputation of being weak or evilly disposed.

Borrowing is the ruin of agricultural nations and the life of manufacturing ones.

The luxuries of the rich give necessaries to the poor.

In the application of laws it is necessary to take into consideration the non-producers.

Our system of jurisprudence is a patchwork. It is not based on comprehensive general principles.

It is a mistake to suppose that the jury system is strongly intrenched in public opinion.

There is nothing requiring that juries shall be selected from the whole body of the population. Why should there be such a hodge-podge, associating men without intelligence with men of education, to the disgust of the latter?

The police invent more than they find.

Every indulgence to culprits suggests complicity.

Strong reasons have been urged both for and against the jury system. But there is no dissimulating the fact that a tyrannical government would have much more success with juries than with judges who are less under their control, and who always would oppose to it more resistance; moreover, the bloodiest tribunals have had juries. If they had been composed of magistrates, mere custom and formalities would have been a rampart against unjust and arbitrary condemnations. The severity which the continual exercise of these functions so frequently brings is not greatly to be feared when the procedure is public, and the defendants are represented by counsel, with the right of argument *(See Note 25)*.

To interpret the law is to corrupt it; lawyers strangle laws.

A magistrate ought to have courage equal to all proofs, and, for example, like Presidents Harley and Mole *(See Note 26)*, be ready to perish in defending the sovereign, the throne, and the laws. The most glorious death would be that of a soldier on the field of honor, if the death of a magistrate in defense of the sovereign, the throne, and the laws, were not more glorious still.

One means of reducing litigation by half would be to pay lawyers only when they won their case. But I have never been able to impress this idea on the Council of State.

Treaties are observed as long as they are in harmony with interests.

I wish that property in mines, once conceded, should become the same as other kinds of property; that contests regarding it should be submitted to the ordinary courts, and that we entrust the duty of thoroughly working the mines to the interest of the individuals who will come to own them in perpetuity. Fathers will be stimulated by the interests of their children. That is the disposition of the human heart. The whole world builds palaces and plants trees for the generations to come. Mine owners would recognize that instead of digging from the surface, it is necessary to drive levels. They will not want to forfeit the advantages of a comprehensive system of future development for a trifling and temporary advantage.

The national character makes it necessary that the liberty of the press be limited to works of a substantial character. Newspapers should be subjected to severe police regulations *(See Note 27)*.

A people which is able to say everything becomes able to do everything.

It is conceivable that among a people where public opinion must influence everything, where it rightfully affects all ministerial acts, and the deliberations of great state councils, that the press should be absolutely free. But our form of government does not call on the people to take part in political affairs. It is the Senate, the Council of State, and the Corps Legislative which think, which speak, and which act for them. In the English system, public opinion controls the government. The press, therefore, ought not to be prevented from criticising ministers, and censuring their acts. The disastrous effects of this are balanced by the institutions and the manners of the nation.

After all, even in England, what benefits result from this license of the press against men in office? Does it reform them? Does it correct their morals? On the contrary, certain to be attacked whatever may be their conduct, the great, acting openly and without scruple, permit the torrent of criticism, and become all the more corrupt.

Newspapers ought to be reduced to handbills.

Diplomacy is the police in grand costume.

Advice to diplomats: In your conversation carefully avoid everything that might offend. Do not utter criticism of any custom, nor write any ridicule. Every people has its own customs, and it is too much the habit of the French to compare everything with their own, and to offer themselves as models. That is a bad step which will hinder your success by rendering you unbearable in every society.

As a woman of the old aristocracy could even give her body to a plebian, and not disclose to him the secrets of the aristocracy, so men accustomed to the usages of good society are alone the only possible ambassadors.

Where treaties are concerned, an ambassador should take advantage of everything to work for the benefit of his country.

I would prefer that French ambassadors should not have any privileges abroad, and that they should be arrested if they did not pay their debts, or if they conspired, rather than give privileges to foreign ambassadors in France where they are more easily able to conspire, because France is a Republic. The people of France are unsophisticated enough. It is not necessary to increase the importance in their eyes of ambassadors whom they already look on as worth ten times as much as another man. It will be better to say nothing about it. The nation already has too much consideration for foreigners.

I do not maintain that the ceremonies of interment should be entirely free to people of small means, for their pride would prevent them from asking this favor. But it should be so that those who have this sort of vanity could gratify it cheaply. I also want the cemeteries embellished with chapels and other customary ornaments.

I want the Bank of France *(See Note 28)* to be just enough in the hands of the government and not too much. I do not ask that it lend the government money, but that it provide facilities for realizing on its revenue cheaply, and at convenient times and places.

It is a sound principle that commands and garrisons should be changed from time to time. The interest of the state requires that there shall be no irremovable places. The thought of unity should be confined to the unity of the Godhead.

Among those who have learned their trades by practice, it is not easy to secure simplicity; the formalities of the Council of State prevented much simplification.

Foreign commerce, infinitely below manufactures and agriculture in its results, arises out of them, while they do not arise out of it. The interest of these three essential bases of the prosperity of nations are divergent, and often opposed to each other. They ought to be aided in the order of their national importance.

The famous doctrine of *laissez faire, laisser passer (See Note 29)*, will prove dangerous if accepted in too literal a manner.

It is necessary to act on this maxim with prudence and discrimination.

It is by comparison and example that agriculture, like all the other arts, must be perfected. In the departments which are still backward in methods of cultivation, the more well-to-do land owners should be induced to send their children to study the methods in use in the departments where agriculture is flourishing; and they can be induced to do so by encomiums and honors.

I attach a great deal of importance, and a high ideal of glory, to the abolition of mendicancy.

The *emigres (See Note 30)* who left France are more interesting than the men of the same class who did not go out, for they had the courage then to make war, and today to make peace.

I want to take up the subject of Receivers General. They get altogether too much. The Receiver General of Aisne, for example, makes more than a hundred thousand francs a year. It is scandalous. Half the Receivers General make that much. The other half make from forty to fifty thousand francs a year at the least.

I seek in vain where to place the limits between the civil and the religious authorities. The existence of such limits is a chimera. We ought to avoid any reawakening of the ancient pretensions of the priests by these discussions. It is not that the priests are greatly to be feared. They have lost their empire never to regain it. The day of their superiority in the sciences has passed to the civil order. But they are a body which has permanent privileges. The authorities ought to handle them with circumspection.

The monks formed the militia of the Pope, and they recognized no other sovereign. For the same reason they were more to be feared by the government than the secular clergy. The government is never embroiled except by them. . . . I respect that which religion respects, but, as a statesman, I am not able to fall in love with the fanaticism of celibacy. Military fanaticism is the only kind which seems to me good for anything. That in time must be destroyed. My principal purpose in establishing a teaching body is to have a means of directing political and moral opinions. This institution will be a guarantee against the reestablishment of the monks. There will be no more talk to me about it.

A bad law enforced, does more good than a good law emasculated by judicial construction.

Every association is a government within the government.

It is necessary to govern colonies with force; but there is no real force without justice.

The colonial system is ended. We must hold firmly to the free navigation of the sea, and to universal freedom of exchange.

We have given all the whites over to the ferocity of the blacks, and we even think the victims ought not to be dissatisfied! Well, if I had been at Martinique *(See Note 31)* I would have been for the English, because, before all, one must save his life. I am for the whites because I am white. I have no other reason, and that is a good one. How was it possible to give freedom to Africans, to men who had no civilization, who did not even know what a colony was, what France was? It is very easy to say that those who wanted liberty for the blacks wanted bondage for the whites; but still, does anyone believe that if the majority of the Convention had known what they were doing, and known the colonies, they would have given freedom to the blacks? No, undoubtedly very few persons were in a position to foresee the results, and a sentiment of humanity always acts powerfully on the imagination. But as a present matter, to cling to these principles still, is not good faith; it is only pride and hypocrisy.

## VII

### CONCERNING RELIGION

THE honest man never doubts the existence of God, for if reason does not suffice to comprehend Him, the instinct of the soul accepts Him. Everything that pertains to the soul is in sympathy with the religious feeling.

There are no men who understand themselves better than soldiers and priests.

Aristocracy is the spirit of the Old Testament, democracy of the New.

I am among those who think that the pains of the next world were imagined as a complement to the insufficient attractions that are offered us there.

The existence of God is attested by everything that appeals to our imagination. And if our eye cannot reach Him it is because

He has not permitted our intelligence to go so far.

Jesus Christ was the greatest republican.

The merit of Mahomet is that he founded a religion without an inferno.

Charity and alms are recommended in every chapter of the Koran as being the most acceptable services, both to God and the Prophet.

It can be said of priests, as has been said of the tongue, that they are the worst of things or the best.

The religious zeal which animates priests, leads them to undertake labors and to brave perils which would be far beyond the powers of one in secular employment.

Conscience is the most sacred thing among men. Every man has within him a still small voice, which tells him that nothing on earth can oblige him to believe that which he does not believe. The worst of all tyrannies is that which obliges eighteen-twentieths of a nation to embrace a religion contrary to their beliefs, under penalty of being denied their rights as citizens and of owning property, which, in effect, is the same thing as being without a country.

The executive authority ought to be very careful not to intermeddle too much with the affairs of the clergy and of the priests. It is better to let the courts act, to oppose robe to robe, pride of profession to pride of profession. Judges, like priests, are, in their way, a kind of a body of theologians. They, also, have their maxims, their rules, and their canons.

Fanaticism must be put to sleep before it can be eradicated.

The philosophy of the gospel is the philosophy of equality, consequently the most favorable to republican government.

Priests, in the genuine spirit of the gospel, ought to contribute to public tranquility by preaching the sound maxims of charity, which are at the foundation of religion and of the gospel.

Fanaticism is always the product of persecution.

To enable parish priests to be truly useful, and to prevent them from making poor use of their ministry, I wish there were added to the course in theology, a course in agriculture, and in the elements of law, and medicine.

Policemen and prisons ought never to be the means used to bring men back to the practice of religion.

You cannot drag a man's conscience before any tribunal, and no one is answerable for his religious opinions to any power on earth.

There is no place in a fanatic's head where reason can enter.

Religious quarrels are not different from political quarrels; for, priests, soldiers, or magistrates, we are all men. These quarrels end by the intervention of some authority strong enough to compel all parties to get together and make up.

Is it not a fact that the Catholic religion appeals more strongly to the imagination by the pomp of its ceremonies than by the sublimity of its doctrines? When you want to arouse enthusiasm in the masses, it is necessary, above all things, to appeal to their eyes.

The sovereignty of the people, liberty, and equality, these are the code of the gospel.

It is contrary to divine right to prevent a man, who needs to work on Sunday the same as other days of the week, from working on Sunday, in order to earn his bread. The government has no right to enact such a law, unless it gives bread gratis to those who have none. For my part, if I undertook to interfere in the matter, I would be more disposed to order that after the hours of service on Sundays, the shops should be opened, and that workmen should take up their work.

In religion everything ought to be free and for the people. The requirement of paying at the door, or of paying for seats, is something revolting. The poor ought not to be punished simply because they are poor in that which consoles them for their poverty. I have never been willing that tickets of admittance to my chapel should be issued. I have always wanted the seats open to the first comers.

The church ought to be in the state, and not the state in the church.

One crushes a religious nation, one does not undermine it.

The populace judges of the power of God by the power of the priests.

I do not see in religion the mystery of the incarnation so much as the mystery of the social order. It introduces into the thought of heaven an idea of equalization, which saves the rich from being massacred by the poor.

It is with water, and not with oil, that theological volcanoes are put out.

A parish priest ought to be a natural peacemaker, the chief moral influence of his people.

Knowledge and history are the enemies of religion.

Fanaticism is not the enemy most to be feared, but atheism.

Religion is, after all, a sort of inoculation, or vaccination, which, in satisfying our love of the marvelous, indemnifies us against charlatans and magicians. Priests are worth more than the Cagliostros *(See Note 32)*, the Kants *(See Note 33)*, and all the dreamers of Germany.

Man's uneasiness is such, that the vagueness and the mystery which religion presents, are absolutely necessary to him.

The atheist is a better subject than the fanatic; one obeys, the other kills.

To fear death is to make profession of atheism.

The intellectual anarchy which we are undergoing is the result of the moral anarchy, the extinction of faith, the negation of principles, which have preceded.

Philosophers vainly strive; they would establish systems, but they search in vain a better doctrine than that of Christianity, which has reconciled man with himself, insured the peace and public order of nations, and at the same time the happiness and the hope of individuals.

Man loves the marvelous. It has an irresistible charm for him. He is always ready to leave that with which he is familiar to pursue vain inventions. He lends himself to his own deception.

Our credulity is a part of the imperfection of our natures. It is inherent in us to desire to generalize, when we ought, on the contrary, to guard ourselves very carefully from this tendency.

Who knows if the happiness of today may not be the misfortune of the morrow? Religion offers consolation in all phases of life. One is less unhappy when one believes. One finds from the very fact of belief, the strength within himself to support unhappiness.

The Christian religion will always be the most solid support of every government clever enough to use it.

# VIII

## WAR

THERE are only two kinds of plans of campaign, the good and the bad. The good fail nearly always through unforeseen circumstances, which often make the bad succeed.

A general must be a charlatan.

Unhappy the general who comes on the field of battle with a system.

The glory and honor of arms must be the first consideration of a general in giving battle, the safety and the conservation of his men is only secondary. But it is often in the audacity, in the steadfastness, of the general that the safety and the conservation of his men is found.

The gesture of a beloved general is worth more than a clever speech.

A military man must have character as well as brains. Men who have brains but little character have no business in the profession of arms. It is like a ship with too much sail for its hull. It is better to have character and not so much brains. Men who are only moderately supplied with brains, but who have character, often succeed in this trade. You have got to have as much base as height. The man who has plenty of brains, and character in the same degree, he is a Caesar, a Hannibal, a Turenne *(See Note 34)*, a Prince Eugene, or a Frederick the Great.

Inevitable wars are always just.

The military principles of Caesar were those of Hannibal, and those of Hannibal were those of Alexander — to hold his forces in hand, not to be vulnerable at any point, to throw all his forces with rapidity on any given point.

The presence of the general is necessary; he is the head, he is everything in an army. It was not the Roman army which reduced Gaul, but Caesar. It was not the Carthaginian army which held the Republican army trembling at the gates of Rome, but Hannibal.

An army which cannot be reenforced is already defeated *(See Note 35)*.

A commander in chief ought to say to himself several times a day: If the enemy should appear on my front, on my right, on my left, what would I do? And if the question finds him uncertain, he is not well placed, he is not as he should be, and he should remedy it.

During a campaign no commander should sleep under a roof; and there should be only one tent, that of the general in chief, necessary on account of the clerical work to be done.

Military science is the calculation of masses on given points.

The force of any army, like momentum in mechanics, is represented by the mass multiplied by the rate of movement. A rapid march adds to the morale of an army; it increases its means of victory.

Nothing is more important in war than singleness in command. So also when war is made against a single power it is only necessary to have a single army, acting according to a single plan, and led by a single chief.

It is imagination which loses battles.

The moment of greatest peril is the moment of victory.

At the beginning of a campaign it is important to consider whether or not to move forward; but when one has taken the offensive it is necessary to maintain it to the last extremity. However skilfully effected a retreat may be, it always lessens the morale of an army, since in losing the chances of success, they are remitted to the enemy. A retreat, moreover, costs much more in men and materials than the bloodiest engagements, with this difference, also, that in a battle the enemy loses practically as much as you do; while in a retreat you lose and he does not.

Changing from the defensive to the offensive, is one of the most delicate operations in war.

An army ought to be ready every moment to offer all the resistance of which it is capable.

Never march by flank in front of an army in position. This principle is absolute.

The keys of a fortress are worth the liberty of its garrison when it has resolved not to surrender itself. Thus it is always more advantageous to grant honorable terms of capitulation to a garrison which has shown a vigorous resistance, than to risk the chances of an assault.

Soldiers ought to be encouraged by all means to remain with the colors. This will be easily accomplished by showing high esteem for old soldiers. Pay ought to be increased with years of service. It is a great injustice not to pay a veteran more than a recruit.

In war, as in love, in order to take a decisive part, one must be right there.

The art of a general of the advance guard or of the rear guard, is, without compromising himself too far, to hold the enemy, to retard him, to delay him three or four hours in making a league. To accomplish these important results is a matter of tactics, and more essential in cavalry command than in infantry, and in advance or rear guard positions than in any other.

In a battle, as in a siege, the art consists in concentrating very heavy fire on a particular point. The line of battle once established, the one who has the ability to concentrate an unlooked for mass of artillery suddenly and unexpectedly on one of these points is sure to carry the day.

Generals who hold fresh troops for the morrow of the battle, are nearly always beaten. One must use all his forces to the very last man, if any purpose is served by it, for on the morrow of a complete success one has no obstacles before him; the force of prestige alone will assure new triumphs to the victor.

Dealing constantly with even the most violent facts, involves less wear on the heart than dealing with abstractions; military men, therefore, have an advantage over lawyers.

There is a joy in danger.

War is a serious game in which a man risks his reputation, his troops, and his country. A sensible man will search himself to know whether or not he is fitted for the trade.

No man will seek epaulettes on the field of battle, when he can get them in an antechamber.

Nothing can excuse a general for profiting by information gained in the service of his country to fight it and deliver its ramparts to foreigners. This is a crime condemned by religion, morality, and honor.

War is a natural state.

A general-in-chief should give repose to neither victors nor vanquished.

There is only one favorable moment in war; talent consists in knowing how to seize it.

Coolness is the greatest quality in a man destined to command.

The mind of a good general ought to resemble in clearness the lens of a field-glass.

He who cannot look over a battlefield with a dry eye, causes the death of many men uselessly.

In war, the chief alone understands the importance of certain things, and he alone is able by his will, and by his superior information, to vanquish and surmount all difficulties.

In war, theory is all right so far as general principles are concerned; but in reducing general principles to practice there will always be danger. Theory and practice are the axis about which the sphere of accomplishment revolves.

There are some cases where the expenditure of men is an economy of blood.

The secret of great battles consists in knowing how to deploy and concentrate at the right time.

Information obtained from prisoners ought to be accepted only at its real value. A soldier sees nothing beyond his own company; and an officer is able, at the most, to give an account of the position, or of the movements, of the division to which his regiment belonged. And the general-in-chief ought to take into consideration the admissions torn from prisoners only when they are consistent with the reports of the advance guard, in order to fortify his conjectures as to the position of the enemy.

The art of war consists in being always able, even with an inferior army, to have stronger forces than the enemy at the point of attack or the point which is attacked *(See Note 36)*.

The praises of enemies are always to be suspected. A man of honor will not permit himself to be flattered by them, except when they are given after the cessation of hostilities.

Prisoners of war do not belong to the power for whom they have fought; they are wholly under the safeguard of the honor and generosity of the nation which has disarmed them.

Read, and re-read the campaigns of Alexander the Great, Hannibal, Caesar, Gustavus Adolphus, Turenne, Prince Eugene, and of Frederick the Great; model yourself after them; that is the only means of becoming a great captain and of surprising the secrets of the art of war. Your genius enlightened by this study, you will then reject every maxim contradictory to those of these great men.

The most desirable quality in a soldier is constancy in the support of fatigue; valor is only secondary.

There are five things which a soldier must never part with: his gun, his cartridges, his haversack, provisions for four days at least, and his trench tool.

Nothing augments a battalion like success.

An army is a nation which obeys.

Policy and morals concur in repressing pillage.

The best soldier is not so much the one who fights as the one who marches.

As a result of holding councils of war there happens what has always happened from the beginning of time, we end by resigning ourselves to the worst, which, in war, is nearly always the most pusillanimous part.

Gentleness, good treatment, honor the victor and dishonor the vanquished, who should remain aloof and owe nothing to pity.

In war, audacity is the finest calculation of genius.

When once the flames of civil war break out, military chiefs are only the means of victory; it is the crowd that governs.

In the wars of parties, defeat permanently discourages; it is therefore in civil wars especially, that good fortune is necessary.

In civil war it is not given to every man to know how to conduct himself. There is something more than military prudence necessary; there is need of sagacity and the knowledge of men.

Give yourself all the chances of success, when you plan to engage in a great battle, especially if your opponent is a great captain; for if you are beaten, if you should be in the midst of your stores, near your fortified places, unhappy the vanquished.

Privation and misery are the real instructors of the soldier.

Nothing is so contrary to military rules as to make the strength of your army known, either in the orders of the day, in proclamations, or in the newspapers. When one is led to speak of his force he should exaggerate their number, making the number formidable by doubling or trebling it; and, on the contrary, when one speaks of the force of the enemy, one ought to diminish their number by a half or a third; all is fair in war.

Courage is like love; it must have hope for nourishment.

War is a lottery in which nations ought to risk nothing but small amounts.

War is above all else an affair of skill.

In war a great disaster always indicates a great culprit.

The man of genius always recovers himself after a fault as after a misfortune.

The French nation has never been vanquished when united.

Our troops go forward spontaneously. A war of invasion pleases them. But a standstill defensive does not fit in with the French genius.

There is but one honorable way to be made a prisoner of war. That is to be taken singly, and without being able to use one's weapons. Then there is nothing else to be done; one yields to necessity.

Achilles was the son of a goddess and of a mortal; in that, he is the image of the genius of war. The divine part is all that that is derived from moral considerations of character, talent, the interest of your adversary, of opinion, of the temper of the soldier, which is strong and victorious, or feeble and beaten, according as he believes this divine part to be. The mortal part is the arms, the fortifications, the order of battle — everything which arises out of material things.

In war any commander of a fortress who yields it a moment sooner than he is obliged to, deserves death.

Alarms dampen spirits and paralyze courage.

When a city is in a state of siege, a military commander becomes a sort of magistrate and must conduct himself with moderation and the decency which the circumstances require.

To violate military agreements is to renounce civilization; it is to put one's self on the level of the Bedouin of the desert.

The principle of all negotiations for an armistice is that each shall remain in the situation in which the armistice finds him. The rights of all follow from the application of this principle.

Of all men, the soldier is the most sensible to benefits.

When a nation has no records for enrollment, and no principle of military organization, it is very hard for it to organize an army.

For the brave a gun is only the handle of a bayonet.

When a soldier has been disgraced and dishonored by being flogged, he cares little for the glory and honor of his country.

Intrepid men are not found among those who have something to lose.

In war, genius is thought in action.

When conscription is no longer looked on as a burden, but only as a point of honor, of which each is jealous, then only is a nation great, glorious, strong; it is then alone that it is in a position to brave reverses, invasions — time itself.

Courage cannot be counterfeited. It is one virtue that escapes hypocrisy.

My custom is to sleep on the battlefield.

In war one must lean on an obstacle in order to overcome it.

No man has a place in the French army who values life more than the national glory and the esteem of his comrades.

A general in the power of the enemy has no more orders to give to those who still fight.

In war, character and opinion make more than half of the reality.

If ever an army invades England, London will not be able to resist an hour.

That dependable courage, which in spite of the most sudden circumstances, nevertheless allows freedom of mind, of judgment and of decision, is exceedingly rare.

Bravery is an innate quality; no one can give it to you, it is in the blood. Courage is a quality of the mind. Bravery is often only impatience of danger.

War is becoming an anachronism; if we have battled in every part of the continent it was because two opposing social orders were facing each other, the one which dates from 1789, and the old regime. They could not exist together; the younger devoured the other. I know very well, that, in the final reckoning, it was war that overthrew me, me the representative of the French Revolution, and the instrument of its principles. But no matter! The battle was lost for civilization, and civilization will inevitably take its revenge. There are two systems, the past and the future. The present is only a painful transition. Which must triumph? The future, will it not? Yes indeed, the future! That is, intelligence, industry, and peace. The past was brute force, privilege, and ignorance. Each of our victories was a triumph for the ideas of the Revolution. Victories will be won, one of these days, without cannon, and without bayonets.

It is not that addresses at the opening of a battle make the soldiers brave. The old veterans scarcely hear them, and recruits forget them at the first boom of the cannon. Their usefulness lies in their effect on the course of the campaign, in neutralizing rumors and false reports, in maintaining a good spirit in the camp, and in furnishing matter for camp-fire talk. The printed order of the day should fulfill these different ends.

One is brave only for others.

What are the conditions that make for the superiority of an army? Its internal organization, military habits in officers and men, the confidence of each in themselves; that is to say, bravery, patience, and all that is contained in the idea of moral means.

The issue of a battle is the result of an instant, of a thought. There is the advance, with its various combinations, the battle is joined, the struggle goes on a certain time, the decisive moment presents itself, a spark of genius discloses it, and the smallest body of reserves accomplish victory.

In war, groping tactics, half-way measures, lose everything.

Europe will never be tranquil until natural limits are restored.

The worst punishment possible in a French army is shame.

A man who has no consideration for the needs of his men ought never to be given command.

Left to themselves, infantry against cavalry would never reach definite results. But with artillery, forces being equal, cavalry ought to annihilate infantry.

An army should be constituted of a just proportion of infantry, cavalry, and artillery. These different arms never take the place of one another. For every thousand men there should be four pieces of artillery, and cavalry equal to a fourth of the infantry.

One ought never to detach troops from an army on the eve of an attack. Conditions change from one moment to another. A battalion may decide the fate of a day.

The infantry is the soul of an army.

The better infantry is, the more necessary it is to handle them well, and to support them with good batteries.

The strength of cavalry is in its impetus. But it is not alone its rapidity which assures success, it is its formation, its organization, and the good employment of its reserves.

Artillery is more necessary to cavalry than to infantry, since cavalry do not return fire, and are not able to fight except with side arms. It is to supplement this lack that horse artillery has been originated. Cavalry ought always to have its batteries with it, whether it attacks, remains in position, or re-forms.

To plan to reserve cavalry for the finish of the battle, is to have no conception of the power of combined infantry and cavalry charges, either for attack or for defense.

It is not necessary to dissimulate; I intend from this time to choose my admirals from among the young officers of thirty-two and thereabouts. I have enough frigate captains with ten years' experience in navigation to be able to choose from among them six, to whom I would be willing to confide commands. My intention is to advance and develop these young men by every possible means.

The art of war on land is an art of genius, of inspiration. In that of the sea there is nothing of genius or inspiration. There, everything is constant and according to experience. The general of the sea has need of only one science, that of navigation. The one on land has need of all, or of a talent which is the equivalent of all, that will enable him to profit by all experience, and all knowledge. A general of the sea has nothing to divine. He knows where his enemy is, he knows his strength. A general on land never knows anything with certainty, never sees his enemy well, and never knows positively where he is.

A general commandant-in-chief of a naval army, and a general commandant-in-chief of an army on land, need very different qualities. One must be born with the qualities necessary for the latter; while the qualities necessary for the former can be acquired only by experience.

A general-in-chief on the sea depends more on his captains of vessels than a general-in-chief on land does on his generals. On land the commander-in-chief has the right, and the opportunity, to himself take direct command of troops, to support every point, and to remedy any false movements. A general of the sea has personal influence only on the men on the vessel on which he happens to be, the smoke preventing signals from being seen on the others. It is therefore, of all callings, that one wherein subalterns must take the most on themselves.

In order not to be astonished at obtaining victories, one ought not to think only of defeats.

The loss of our naval battles arose from the lack of force in the generals-in-chief, to their defects of tactics, and to the belief held by the captains that they ought to act only in accordance with signals.

On land, an undisciplined bravery has been able to win sometimes; on the sea, never.

We celebrate a victory, even while we weep over the fallen, even enemies.

In war, luck is half in everything.

My most splendid campaign was that of March 20; not a single shot was fired *(See Note 37).*

I have a hundred thousand pensioners.

# IX

## SOCIOLOGY

OUR light-heartedness, lack of reflection, comes to us honestly. We will always be Gauls. We will not place a true value on things until we substitute principles for turbulence, pride for vanity, and love of institutions for love of places.

In France, only the impossible is admired.

I have shown France what she is capable of; let her achieve it.

The distinctive characteristic of our nation is that we are much too mercurial in prosperity.

The French people have two equally powerful passions which seem the very opposites of each other, but which, nevertheless, grow out of the same sentiment. They are the love of equality and the love of distinctions. A government can satisfy these two needs only by exact justice. The law and the operation of government should be equal for all, and honors and rewards should come to those men who, in the eyes of all, seem most worthy.

The sentiment of national honor is never more than half extinguished in the French. It takes only a spark to re-kindle it.

The Emperor observed that we French, if we had less energy than the Romans, had more decency. We would not have killed ourselves, as they did, under the first Emperors, but we would not have shown all the turpitude, all the servility, that was displayed under the last. "Even in our most corrupt moments," said he, "our baseness was not without a certain reserve."

The French nation is easily governed if one does not get at cross purposes with it. Nothing equals its quick and easy comprehension. It distinguishes, instantly, those who work for it, and those who work against it. The appeal must always be made to its intelligence. Otherwise its inquiet spirit frets itself, it ferments and explodes.

Credulity has been the national characteristic of the French since the time of the Gauls.

If the Roman people had made the same use of their strength that the French people have of theirs, the Roman Eagles would still surmount the Capital, and eighteen centuries of slavery and of tyranny would not have dishonored the human species.

Without a navy, France is exposed to all sorts of insults.

Every system finds apologists in France.

The French complain of everything, and always.

France loves change too much for any government to endure there.

With a sincere ally, France will be mistress of the world.

When I learn that a nation can live without bread, then I will believe that the French people can live without glory.

The French are, perhaps, the only nation in which all ranks of society, can be moved equally strongly by means of honor.

I would like the title of Frenchman to be the finest, the most desirable, in the world; that every Frenchman traveling anywhere in Europe should believe himself, should find himself, always among friends.

There is nothing which you cannot get from the French by the lure of danger. It seems to give them spirit.

It is a part of the French character to exaggerate, to complain, and to distort everything when dissatisfied.

Among the English, the higher classes have pride; among us, unfortunately, they have only vanity. Herein is the great and characteristic difference between the two people. The great mass of our people, today at least (1816), constitute that people of Europe in which the national sentiment is strongest. It has profited by its twenty-five years of revolution; but, unfortunately, the class which the Revolution has raised has not responded in any degree to its new destinies. It has shown only corruption and versatility. It has displayed in these last crises neither talent nor character nor virtue. It has lost the honor of the nation *(See Note 38)*.

Valor, the love of glory, is an instinct, a sort of sixth sense, with the French. Many a time in the heat of battle, my attention has been arrested by the sight of a young conscript, in his first engagement, throwing himself into the struggle. Honor and courage seemed to exude from every pore.

France will always be a great nation.

The Turks can be killed, but they can never be conquered.

No one saw in my war in Spain the possession of the Mediterranean.

Europe is a molehill. It has never had any great empires, like those of the Orient, numbering six hundred million souls.

Antwerp is ever a loaded pistol aimed at the heart of England.

England is the only power whose interest it is that France shall not have Belgium; and as long as England will not allow France to possess that country, there is no sincerity in her alliance.

Whoever possesses Constantinople ought to rule the world.

When the Russians make themselves masters of Constantinople, they will be able to retain as many Moslems there as they care to, by assuring them of their property rights, and tolerating their religion. The Moors of Spain submitted to everything, even the inquisition, and it took an order from Ferdinand and Isabella to expel them.

I have inplanted in the Italians principles which will never be eradicated, but which will go on forever working out their natural results.

It will take a skilful legislator to develop a taste for arms among the Italians.

One of my cherished thoughts has been to reunite and reestablish, geographically, the peoples which revolutions and politics have broken up and parcelled out. There are in Europe thirty million French, fifteen million Spaniards, fifteen million Italians, thirty million Germans, and twenty million Poles; I would make of each, one nation. The impulse has been given, each of these results will be accomplished; and it is my thought which will have served the future destiny of Europe *(See Note 39)*.

Europe has its history, often tragic, though at intervals consoling. But to speak of any universally recognized national rights or that these rights have played any part in its history, is to play with the powers of public credulity. Always the first duty of a state has been its safety; the pledge of its safety, its power; and the limits of its power, that intelligence of which each has been made the depository. When the great powers have proclaimed any other principle, it has been only for their own purposes, and the smaller powers have never received any benefit from it. Poland, Venice, have disappeared from the earth as states, while the assembled spectators have seen in these political funerals nothing but their own loss. Whenever there has been a partition of spoils, or compensation given in lieu of them, there has been no suggestion of ambition. But these compensations, though they have always been exacted in the name of justice, have always, in fact, been in the name of force. That is all there is of reality in the pretended European Code. That is what our modern statesmen have called their "balance of power," a ridiculous term which, to the wars engendered by pure ambition, has added other wars. It is a mistaken theory which has furnished pretext for many iniquities, but which has saved the weak, only when the strong have not known just how to get around it. From this so-called great principle there have followed two things, each historically true. One is that each state claims the right to control interests foreign to itself when those interests are such that it can control them without putting its own interests in danger. The other principle is that the other powers only recognize this right of intervening in proportion as the country doing it has the power to do it.

# NOTES

*Note* 1.— Napoleon gave the seal of sincerity to this extremely cynical philosophy, by his ejaculation, "Oh, well; a rival the less," when told of the death of General Kleber by assassination in Cairo, June 14, 1800. Kleber was undoubtedly one of the greatest generals of the French revolutionary epoch.

*Note* 2.— This is generally looked on as Napoleon's own idealization and defense of himself and of his seizure of power, the successive steps by which he sought to make himself the founder of a dynasty, and of the despotic character of his government.

*Note* 3.— Acting, at least to some extent, in the spirit here enunciated, Napoleon in 1802 instituted the Order of the Legion of Honor. All previously existing French military or religious orders — those of St. Michael, the Holy Ghost, St. Louis, and Military Merit, as well as the united orders of St. Lazarus and Our Lady of Mount Carmel had been abolished at the Revolution. The Legion of Honor survived the restoration of the Bourbons, indeed was adopted by them, though modified in some particulars, while the old orders were restored. It has maintained itself through all political changes, and since the establishment of the Third Republic has been the only military order in France — for it is essentially military in character, though not strictly confined to the recognition of military merit. It is conferred for distinguished services of any kind, and is not limited to citizens of France. The order has occasionally been conferred on women, as for instance on Rosa Bonheur, the painter, and on Madame Curie, who with her husband discovered radium.

*Note* 4.— The necessity for a code in France grew out of the immense number of separate systems of jurisprudence existing in the country before 1789, justifying Voltaire's sarcasm that a traveler in France had to change laws about as often as he changed horses. The conception of a general code for the whole country had occurred to statesmen and jurists before Napoleon; and the Convention, in fact, discussed two projects presented by Cambaceres, one of which had been found too complicated and the other too condensed.

Napoleon, on becoming Consul, appointed a commission headed by M. Tronchet to review previous efforts and to present a new project. In four months the project was presented to the government, submitted to the judges, and discussed by the Council of State — Napoleon himself taking part in the deliberations. At first published under the title of Code Civil des Francais, it was afterwards called the Code Napoleon — the Emperor wishing to attach his name to a work which he regarded as the greatest glory of his reign.

The Code Napoleon consists of 2,281 articles, arranged under titles and divided into three books, preceded by a preliminary title. The subjects of the different books are, first, "Des Personnes"; second, "Des biens et des differents modifications de la propriete"; third, "Des differents manieres d'acquerir la propriete." It has passed through several changes caused by the political vicissitudes of the country, and it has, of course, suffered from time to time important alterations in substance, but it still remains virtually the same in principle as it left the hands of its framers.

The remaining French codes are the "Code de Procedure civile," "Code de Commerce," "Code d'instruction criminelle," and the "Code penal."

The merits of the Code Napoleon have entered into the discussion on the general subject of codification. Austin agrees with Savigny in condemning the ignorance and haste with which it was compiled. "It contains," says Austin, "no definitions of technical terms (even the most leading), no exposition of the rationale of distinctions (even the most leading), no exposition of the broad principles and rules to which the narrower provisions in the code are subordinate — hence its fallacious brevity." All the French Codes have, however, taken firm root in most of the continental countries of Europe. Introduced by French conquest, they nevertheless were eagerly adopted by the people after the French arms had been withdrawn.

*Note* 5.— Henry IV (1553–1610), son of Antony of Bourbon, King of Navarre, and Jeanne of Albret, was, on his father's side, the tenth in descent from Saint Louis. He was brought up a Calvinist by his mother. In 1571 he married Margaret of Valois, daughter of Catherine de Medici. He escaped the massacre of St. Bartholomew only by professing Catholicism, but on his escape from court in 1575 he became the acknowledged head of the Huguenots, and by his dashing bravery kept life in their dispirited forces. He had all the qualities of a guerilla leader, though he was not a great general. His conversion to Catholicism in 1593 proved of great political advantage, and by 1598 he had overcome all important opposing influences. He issued the Edict of Nantes in April, 1598, and from that time on devoted his energies to the restoration of the country devastated by nearly forty years of civil war. The organizing genius of Maximilian of Bethune, Duke of Sully, restored the finances, and agriculture, manufactures, and commerce made marvelous advances.

Henry was assassinated by Ravaillac, May 14, 1610.

Philip IV, known as Philip the Fair, King of France, was born in 1268 and died in 1314. His was a troubled reign, including a controversy with Pope Boniface VIII; and while Philip the Fair in his personality does not challenge our sympathy, he stands as one of the great figures in French history. He is thought of as the first sovereign in the modern sense. He made himself the head of both the temporal power and the church in France, freed himself in large degree from the feudal lords, increased the royal domain, and greatly developed both administrative and judicial institutions.

*Note* 6.— Voltaire, whose real name was Francois Marie Arouet, was born in Paris in 1694 and died there in 1778. He began to call himself Arouet de Voltaire, or simply Voltaire, after his release from the Bastille in April, 1718. His father was a prosperous notary from whom he inherited a comfortable fortune; and Voltaire, himself, had the money-making ability, not wholly free from unscrupulousness, and amassed a considerable fortune. To his own age Voltaire was preeminently a poet and philosopher. Later ages have questioned whether he was entitled to either name. But he exercised a wonderful influence on his own century, an influence that was in many aspects very largely beneficial. Throughout his whole life he was the opponent of intolerance, especially of religious and political intolerance. No other writer has written on as great a variety of subjects as he, nor as much, and everything he wrote was French in its limpid clearness, elegance, precision, and purity of style. The most diametrically opposite opinions have been held of him, but there can be little doubt that he was one of the great men not only of his time but of all times.

*Note* 7.— The Encyclopedists is a name by which the world designates that wonderful body of men, D'Alembert, Diderot, Voltaire, Montesquieu, Rousseau, and their associates, who wrote, edited and otherwise prepared that marvelous work, the French *Encyclopedia,* published during the period from 1751 to 1772. No encyclopedia perhaps has been of such political importance, or has occupied so conspicuous a place in the civil and literary history of its century. It sought not only to give information but to guide opinion. It was theistic but heretical.

It was opposed to the church, then all powerful in France, and it treated dogma historically. It was a war machine. As it progressed, its attacks both on the church and on the still more despotic government, became bolder and more undisguised, and it was met by opposition and persecution unparalleled in the history of encyclopedias. The preliminary discourse by D'Alembert printed with the first volume gives an admirable and comprehensive view of the scope and extent of human knowledge as it existed at the period immediately preceding the French Revolution, and from this point of view is the most important philosophic work of the eighteenth century. The *Encyclopedia* in many ways prepared the way for the Revolution by spreading knowledge, awakening inquiry and intelligence, and by the direction it gave to thought regarding human rights.

*Note* 8.— Fenelon, Francois de Salignac de la Mothe, Archbishop of Cambray and one of the most celebrated names in the intellectual and ecclesiastical history of France in the seventeenth century, was born August 6, 1651, and died January 17, 1715. He came of a family ennobled from the middle of the fifteenth century which gave many distinguished names to France. He became the preceptor of the young Duke of Burgundy, a violent and impetuous, but affectionate and bright child, whom he developed into a well-disciplined and promising youth whose life, if spared, might have brought blessing to France.

For the instruction of his pupil, Fenelon wrote, among other things, his celebrated *Telemaque*. In this his enemies saw covert criticisms of the government of Louis XIV, and the publication of this work resulted in his losing the royal favor. Out of the Quietist doctrines, championed by Madame Guyon, which he scrupled to condemn, there grew a bitter controversy with Bossuet, and Fenelon was condemned by the Holy See. He submitted to this decision and spent the remainder of his life in his diocese in ceaseless works of Christian piety and charity, becoming more honored in his retirement than he had been in Paris.

Fenelon is chiefly remembered for the beauty of his character, his tender and mystic devotion, and the charm of his style as a writer. He is not great as a thinker, nor can the substance of his writings be said to have a permanent value. But there is the same subtle delicacy, sensibility, tenderness, and purity of expression in his style as in his character. An exquisite, highly-toned, and noble genius pervades the one as the other. As a man he is one of the greatest figures in a great time. As a writer he has been placed in prose on the same level with Racine in poetry. In both there is the same full harmony and clearness, the same combination of natural grace with perfect art.

*Note* 9.—Jean de la Fontaine was born in 1621 and died in 1695. His fame as a poet is based on his tales and his fables. The latter have an irresistible charm and have become universal property, accepted by every age since his. They touch the most diverse human qualities, but always with delicious originality. They are veritable creations. No one has rivaled him in the exquisite grace, the malicious good humor, the simplicity, and naturalness with which he makes the personages of his fables speak, nor in the perfect art of his style. While in these fables he has given expression to a few sentiments of personal egotism, on the whole his works bear the imprint of the engaging sweetness, the innocent kindliness, and the sensibility of his nature.

*Note* 10.—Jean Racine, celebrated French tragic poet, was born in 1639 and died in 1699. He was the friend of Boileau, La Fontaine, and Moliere. In some respects the rival of Corneille, his works are gentler, nearer nature, and more human in their touch. While Corneille sought complicated plots within which his heroes deployed their superhuman qualities, Racine sought simple, clear plots, in which the delineation of passions in simple fidelity to truth was his effort. His influence on the French language of his time was both extensive and beneficial. Among his principal tragedies are, ***Andromaque, Britannicus, Mithridate, Iphigenie,*** and ***Phedre,*** and the sacred tragedies, ***Esther,*** and ***Athalie.***

*Note* 11.—*Tartuffe* is a comedy in five acts by Moliere, and the masterpiece of French comedy. Tartuffe, the chief character, will always remain the type of perversity and dissimulated corruption under an exterior of respectability; in other words, of hypocrisy. Many passages of the comedy have passed into the language as proverbs.

*Note* 12.— *Gil Blas* is one of the most celebrated romances in literature. It was written by Alain Rene le Sage, a Frenchman (1668–1747), the creator of the romance of manners. Gil Blas, the hero of the story, has become the type of the well-brought-up and instructed young man living constantly by expedients more or less doubtful, and who is constantly throwing himself into new adventures.

*Note* 13.— Francois Rene de Chateaubriand, an illustrious French writer (1768–1848), traveled in America, returning to France just as the Revolution began. He became an *emigre* in 1792. After the Restoration he was minister of foreign affairs. The most salient qualities of his style are brilliancy, wealth of imagination, and a gorgeous eloquence. He exercised a considerable influence on the development of romantic literature. Posterity has not found the same value in his writings that his contemporaries did. *The Genius of Christianity* is the work by which he is best known to English readers.

*Note* 14.— Jean Francois de la Harpe (1739–1803), was a French poet and literary critic. Among others of his works is a *Cours de Litterature,* which is excellent, especially for the seventeenth century.

*Note* 15.— Madame de Staël (1766–1817), was the daughter of the famous financier Necker. Her husband was Eric Magnus, Baron of Stael-Holstein, Ambassador of Sweden to France. Her marriage was largely one of convenience. Her husband obtained money, and she a position; but there was no scandal. They had three children. She was ambitious for power and influence in a noisy extravagant way, though honest and sincere in her political convictions, which were liberal. Just why there should have been the bitterness between Napoleon and herself it is hard to say. She was a woman of influence, and it doubtless displeased Napoleon that she should show herself recalcitrant to his influence. But it also doubtless pleased Madame de Staël to quite an equal degree, that Napoleon should apparently put forth his power to crush her and fail. Napoleon's course toward her was little creditable to him. He exiled her from France and he suppressed her book *Germany,* after it had been passed by the censor. Coppet is a Swiss village on the Lake of Geneva where she made her home during much of her exile. Her books, of which *Corinne* and *Delphine* are probably the best known, were given extravagant praise during her life, but are now little read. Her son edited an edition of her writings in seventeen volumes. She counted among those whom she greatly influenced, Benjamin Constant, Schlegel, Talleyrand, Narbonne, Jaucourt, Guibert, Byron, and many others. She was a remarkable woman in many ways, and as Napoleon said, "she will endure."

*Note* 16.—Armide and Clorinde, or, as they are known under the English spelling, Armida and Clorinda, are two characters in Tasso's *Jerusalem Delivered.* Armida, seductively beautiful, who was sent forth by the infernal senate to sow discord in the Christian camp, turns the action of the epic. Her name is often used to designate a woman who fascinates by her seductive charms. Clorinda, on the other hand, bravely donning armor, like Marfisa, fights in duel with her devoted lover, receives baptism from his hands in her pathetic death, and has become the type of the courageous woman who scorns the fears and weaknesses so natural to her sex.

*Note* 17.— Pierre Augustin, Caron de Beaumarchais, was born in Paris in 1732 and died in 1799. He was the author of *The Barber of Seville, The Marriage of Figaro,* and *Mére Coupable,* all of them audacious dramas, sparkling with witty lines, full of movement and gaiety. Beaumarchais was audacious and adventurous in character, and he has left some remarkable and curious *Memoirs,* the material for which grew largely out of his controversies with Counsellor Goezman.

*Note* 18.— The Theatre Francaise, or as it has for a long time been known, the Comedie Francaise, was founded by Louis XIV in 1680. It had exclusive rights until the Revolution, when the liberty of the theatre, among other liberties, was proclaimed; and there were soon no less than fifty theatres in Paris. In 1807 the Empire restricted the number to nine, and reinstated the Theatre Francaise in sole possession (or nearly such) of the right of performing the classic drama.

*Note* 19.— The Chateau, or Palace, of Versailles was designed by Mansard for Louis XIV.

It was the favorite residence of the Bourbons for a hundred years. The States-General met here in May, 1789, and from this meeting dates the French Revolution. The King of Prussia was proclaimed Emperor of Germany here in 1871. It was the residence of the President of the French Republic from 1871 to 1879. Louis Phillipe restored the palace to its ancient splendor. It is one of the showplaces of France and is visited annually by thousands.

*Note* 20.— In 1789 the Constituent Assembly proclaimed that all authority emanated from the nation, and that there was no authority in France superior to the law. Conceiving that the persistence of the old provinces with their variety of local customs might be an obstacle to the thorough working out of this idea, it abolished these provinces, as administrative divisions, and divided France into eighty-three departments which were administered by locally elective officials for a time. The Revolutionary Government took some of their power away from these, appointing a commissioner of its own in each department. When Napoleon became First Consul, all elective representation in the department was abolished and a prefect was appointed by him for each. These prefects, each in his own department, controlled the entire departmental administration: Conscription, taxation, agriculture, commerce, public works, education, and charity — "everything relating to the public wealth, the national prosperity, and the peace of those under your Administration," as a circular of instructions to prefects issued at the time, expressed it. This system prevailed under the Consulate, the Empire, and the Restoration. Decentralization and local representation in departmental affairs began in 1830 and were extended after the revolution of 1848, and still further under the Republic. Though the prefect has lost much of his former power, he is still an important functionary. He represents the national government; he has a certain veto or restraining power over mayors and municipal councils; he is responsible for the public order; he can call for troops to suppress riots; his regulations regarding matters coming within the scope of his authority have the force of law; and he has the appointment of a large number and variety of minor functionaries and public employes, including the teachers in the public schools.

*Note* 21.— The Battle of Rossbach was fought November 5, 1757, between 25,000 Prussians, under Frederick the Great, and 64,000 French and Imperial troops — the French under the Duke of Soubise and the Imperial troops under the Prince of Hildburghausen. It was one of the decisive battles of "The Seven Years War."

*Note* 22.— The body known as the University of Paris was founded about 1150, and from its beginning had very great privileges. It alone had the control and direction of public instruction, and in addition had jurisdiction in other particulars. On numerous occasions it took part in public affairs. It defended the liberties of the Church in France, and carried on long struggles against certain religious orders. The University was suppressed in 1790, but was reorganized by Napoleon in 1808. He put at the head of it a Grand Master, and placed it directly under the control of the state; and France was territorially divided into six academies, each presided over by a Rector. At the present time the name Universities is given to the several bodies, which, each in its own division of France, has direction and control of higher education. These bodies are all united in a Council of the University, of which the Minister of Public Instruction is Grand Master.

*Note* 23.— The Lycees are a system of free schools for secondary instruction. They were founded in Paris in 1787 for instruction in literature and science.

*Note* 24.— *La Gabelle* was a tax on salt, a part of a system of state salt monopoly under the ancient régime in France. The price of salt varied in different provinces. Each individual was obliged to buy a certain amount of salt, resulting in much that was vexatious in the enforcement of the tax and the monopoly. This salt tax was fully established in 1340 and was abolished in 1789 with many other tyrannies and abuses by the spirit of equality and freedom which brought about the French Revolution.

*Note* 25.— In France the institution of juries in criminal cases dates from 1791. It was one of the fruits of the French Revolution, and in the action and reaction of opinion that surged so violently during the years immediately following, it had hardly had time to become a firmly fixed institution in Napoleon's day.

*Note* 26.— Achille de Harlay, President of the Parliament of Paris, was born in Paris in 1536. He died in 1619. Matthieu Mole (1584–1656), President of the Parliament of Paris, and Keeper of the Seal, played an important rôle during the Fronde. He negotiated the Peace of Ruel early in 1649.

*Note* 27.— At the Revolution the restrictions on the freedom of the press were swept away, the Assembly declaring it to be the right of every citizen to print and publish his opinions. The press remained effectually free in France until the Law of February 5, 1810, secured by Napoleon, established a direction of the press. The restrictions on the freedom of the press continued to be a factor, in some degree, of every change in the form of government from that time to the establishment of the Third Republic, when liberty of the press was completely reestablished.

*Note* 28.— The Bank of France, which had been founded in 1799, was definitely organized by the law of April 26, 1806, which gave the management of the bank to a governor and two deputy governors, appointed by the chief of the state, and assisted by a council of fifteen regents and three censors, elected by the shareholders. In addition to issuing bank notes which circulate as freely as gold, the bank has all the usual banking powers, and transacts a wide variety of commercial and financial functions. It is the great instrument of credit in France. By loans in difficult circumstances it has more than once supported the government, which owns a large number of its shares.

*Note* 29.—*Laissez faire, laissez passer,* was the maxim into which Gournay (1712–1759), one of the leading members of that school of political economists known as the Physiocrats, condensed his doctrine of industrial freedom, which is that trade and industry and every guiltless exercise of individual will should be left free from taxation or restriction or interference by government, except so far as is required by public peace and order. No English translation of the French expression conveys any idea of the economic doctrine it embodies; and thus the expression itself, usually abridged to *laissez faire* has been adopted into our language as the term by which this doctrine is identified or understood.

*Note* 30.—*Emigres* is a name given to those members of the French aristocracy, or more exactly to those partisans of the old régime, who fled from France beginning within a few days after the fall of the Bastille, July 14, 1789. The *emigres* appealed to foreign governments and brought about armed invasion of their own country.

*Note* 31.—The Island of Martinique is one of the Lesser Antilles, and has been a French possession, with short interruptions, for nearly three hundred years. African slave labor was early introduced, and by 1736 there were 72,000 blacks.

Slavery was abolished by the Convention in the early course of the French Revolution, and in 1794 the island was taken possession of by the English under Sir John Jervis and Sir Charles Grey, and retained for eight years, and it is of this action that Napoleon speaks. The Empress Josephine was born in Martinique in 1763.

*Note* 32.— Joseph Balsamo, Count of Cagliostro, an Italian occultist, physician, and clever charlatan, was born at Palermo, about 1743. He had a successful career at the court of Louis XVI and in Parisian society. He died in 1795.

*Note* 33.— Emmanuel Kant (1724–1804), one of the greatest of philosophers, was the grandson of a Scotchman who settled in East Prussia. He was born at Konigsberg. He is best known by his *Critique of Pure Reason.*

*Note* 34.— Turenne (1611–1675) was one of France's greatest captains. In character he was very simple, very modest. His military genius utilized careful calculations and deep study and thought. His memoirs have been published and their value to students of military matters is very great.

*Note* 35.— This is the philosophical summing up of Napoleon's experience in Egypt. Nelson's victory of the Nile, lost to Napoleon and the French the control of the Mediterranean. The Directory was no longer able to reenforce him. In no way could he make up for the losses to his army which even victories entailed. His army became smaller and smaller; but, with that genius for success which was the mainspring of his destiny, Napoleon, after the Acre campaign, seized the right moment and a plausible reason for transferring the command to the less subtle Kleber, and himself returned to France with the luster of success not wholly dimmed, to embrace opportunity, and command armies still animated and recruited by the Republican youth of France.

*Note* 36.—General Forrest, the brilliant cavalry leader of the Confederacy, is said to have expressed this guiding principle by declaring that the way to win was to "get there first with the most men."

*Note* 37.—By the campaign of March 20, Napoleon refers to the events following his return from Elba and his arrival at Paris. He landed March 1, 1815, between Cannes and Antibes, and twenty days later entered the Tuileries in triumph. Louis XVIII left the Tuileries March 19, and on the next day Napoleon entered Paris.

*Note* 38.—Napoleon at this time had not been long at St. Helena. It was still fresh in his memory that after his abdication June 22, 1815, in favor of his son, the Chamber of Representatives passed this son over, and named an executive commission of five, the Bourbons, in the person of Louis XVIII, thus being restored.

*Note* 39.—This utterance of Napoleon acquires a particular significance at this time when, as a result of the war between Germany and Austria on the one side, and Russia, France, and Great Britain on the other, so much has been said and is being said of the possibility, as a result of this war, of just what Napoleon expressed the desire to do.

LaVergne, TN USA
14 December 2009
167027LV00004B/166/A